A FALCON

M000188724

the Pacific Northwest
Berry Book

A complete guide to finding, harvesting, and preparing

wild berries and fruits in the Pacific Northwest.

Includes 107 recipes and 47 color photos.

Bob Krumm and James Krumm

FALCON®
Helena, Montana

©1998 by Falcon® Publishing, Inc., Helena, Montana
Printed in Canada.

1 2 3 4 5 6 7 8 9 0 TP 03 02 01 00 99 98

All rights reserved, including the right to reproduce any part of this book in any form, except brief quotations for reviews, without the written permission of the publisher.

Front cover photo by Bob Krumm.

All photos in the color section are Bob Krumm's, unless otherwise noted.

Library of Congress Cataloging-in-Publication Data

Krumm, Bob, 1944–
    The Pacific Northwest berry book : a complete guide to finding,
    harvesting, and preparing wild berries and fruits in the Pacific
    Northwest / Bob Krumm and James Krumm.
            p.   cm.
    Includes indexes.
    ISBN 1-56044-681-1 (paperback)
    1. Cookery (Berries)   2. Berries—Northwest, Pacific.   3. Berries—
    Harvesting—Northwest, Pacific.   I. Krumm, James, 1971–.
    II. Title
    TX813.B4K788   1998
    641.6'4713—DC21   98-3819
                                                   CIP

♻ Text pages printed on recycled paper.

CONTENTS

ACKNOWLEDGMENTS

To write a book like this one requires a lot of cooperation and help from many people.

Of course there are some persons easy to identify, like my parents, Donald and Emily Krumm. They taught me a lot about the out-of-doors—not just hunting and fishing, but a lot about the flora and fauna. They shared a lot of their outdoor education with me, and I'll always be grateful for that.

Dot Heggie, a long-time friend, got me started writing the berry book series. It was her vision and belief that pushed me into believing that I could write a book. She felt that my books were needed by people who wanted to enjoy the out-of-doors more fully.

My son James, who co-authored this book and did the illustrations, was a great help in supplying the botanical and ecological information used here. He and his brother, Clint, have also blessed me with their love and support, and even willingly accompany me on berry-picking trips nowadays.

Dave Hughes and Masako Tani took off time from hectic writing schedules to show Dot and me their outdoor world near Portland. Masako cooked several fine meals for us and showed us how to pick up a storm. Dave not only guided us about the area, but wrote the foreword for this book.

Pat and Larry Robinson, two complete strangers until we knocked on their door, have become good friends. They ushered us around Washington and took us to their favorite berry patches. Up until I met Pat, I thought I was a berry good picker, but Pat is the champion berry picker of Washington. Pat was very instrumental in compiling a long list of recipes.

Other people have helped immensely. Carol Horvath, Mount Hood National Forest, gave me help regarding species distribution and also pointed me to another botanist, Scott Sundberg, of Oregon State University. Scott took time out from his work on the Oregon Flora Project to answer my questions on species distribution and abundance.

A shirttail relative in McCall, Idaho, Bob Krumm, helped me by sending me a bunch of recipes and referring Darcy Williamson to me. Darcy's recipes helped to round out and fill up many of my chapters. Darcy has written numerous books on preparing wild foods. Her latest book is entitled *Rocky Mountain Wild Food Cookbook.*

My good friend Alma Snell, a Crow Indian medicine woman and granddaughter of Pretty Shield, gave me some useful recipes as well as her prayers. Alma has encouraged me throughout the years and has willingly shared her recipes. If you ever care to learn more about medicinal plants, she is a must to contact in Fort Smith, Montana.

Then there are the people at Falcon Press who have encouraged me to write this book. My thanks and appreciation go to Megan Hiller for her patience and prodding. Thanks, too, to Chris Cauble for his support.

Finally, thanks to the people who helped in a myriad ways. The Sheridan County Fulmer Public Library, and in particular, Jeanne Sanchez, helped me locate the reference texts that I needed. There are folks who volunteered a recipe, offered a word of encouragement, and helped by recounting their berry-picking adventures. Anyway, thanks to all who helped. And to all who buy this book, may your enjoyment be berry good.

FOREWORD

I grew up along the coast of Oregon, in a family that spent summer weekends bouncing along logging roads in a '52 Chevy pickup, scouting for berry patches that sprang up in clearcuts. We were always on the hunt for new patches. The fruits were mountain blackberries or tart red and blue huckleberries that swung home in tin buckets to become pies, cobblers, and sweet jellies or jams.

Mom was infinitely patient in a berry patch. I was not. My greatest discovery was an acre of huckleberries alongside a favorite trout stream. I was able to fish without guilt any summer evening I wanted, merely by dropping Mom in the patch, then dashing upstream in a shower of spray, fly rod in hand.

A black bear left sign that it had picked the same patch. This didn't bother Mom. I returned from fishing early one evening and entered the patch thrashing, then realized that I sounded about like a bear. Mom, deeply embedded in the patch, was poised for flight when I sang out a verse of, "Let's go tell Mommy we put beans in our ears." I became forever after, when we went berry picking together, the bear that put beans in its ears.

My wife, Masako, was born and raised in the center of Tokyo, and is now an outdoor correspondent for Japanese magazines. I'll never know how she inherited the berry-picking gene, but the only way I've found to get her to leave a patch is to con her out of her bucket by promising to bring an empty one from the pickup. She'll emerge later with pockets bulging and hands overflowing.

When Bob Krumm, whom I know better as a fly fishing guide, asked to visit and pick berries with us for a couple of days, I calculated it was a good chance to combine berry picking with fishing once again. Masako and I had discovered a red huckleberry patch, but no other berries, almost drooping over a nearby stream that we fished one evening a week. That's where we took Bob.

Before the day ended he discovered eight kinds of wild berries that we had overlooked. The most embarrassing was a tendril of wild mountain blackberries that led to another tendril, and on and on to others as they always do. He spotted the first of them growing in the grass where we had our picnic dinner every time we finished fishing the stream. We'd nearly sat on them half a dozen times.

The next day we went into unexplored territory—for us—high on the slopes of Mount Hood, about an hour into the Cascade Mountains east of our home in Portland. We stopped in a few timbered places, where Bob pointed out a scattering of new kinds of berries. Then we took a road toward a trout lake near the summit. The trees opened out so the sun could strike in. Bob suddenly said, "I see huckleberries." I stopped, we all got out, and Bob hunted down the berry he'd spotted. It was about 50 feet from the road, hidden beneath a leaf, invisible to any but the most predaceous berry-picking eye. It led us into a vast patch of sun-sweet berries, no more than a mile from a lake where trout rose.

The baby was in day care that day, so we had to get down off the mountain, creep through rush-hour traffic, and pick her up before they closed the doors. We didn't leave early, and we would not have left at all, had I not conned both Masako and Bob out of their buckets, which were overflowing anyway.

Now if you'll excuse me, I've got to go tie some flies. It's winter, but I want to be ready when it's time to drop Masako off in that big berry patch and launch myself into the nearby lake. You turn the page, go berry picking with Bob. He'll expertly show you how to find them, gather them, and most important, make something great out of them once you've got them.

Dave Hughes, author of *Western Streamside Guide* and *Big Indian Creek*
Portland, Oregon

INTRODUCTION

It seems that I have picked berries all my life. As a child I traipsed along with my parents as they went for a Sunday picnic, but the picnic could never be just that. My mother would make sure that we availed ourselves of nature's bounty. While I would have much rather fished or chased frogs, I was coerced into picking berries, something I hated to do. When I aged a little, and I realized that those berries would always lead to some sort of tasty treat—pies, muffins, jam, or jelly—I changed my outlook on berry picking. I became an avid berry picker.

I moved away from my home in Michigan in 1966 to attend the University of Wyoming. Initially, I thought that many of the outdoor activities I took pleasure in were closed to me, but it didn't take me too long to figure out that Wyoming held a lot of outdoor opportunities similar to Michigan's, but also some new ones.

The hunting and fishing were certainly better in Wyoming than in my home state, but the berry picking was a little sparse until I looked more closely. Berries that we neglected to pick in Michigan were highly prized and sought after in Wyoming. Berry species I had never heard of became prized. I found that Wyoming could keep me happy with a bounty of berries.

On July 1, 1995, my son James married a wonderful woman, Tonya Hubbard, and moved to Portland, Oregon, where Tonya worked on completing her degree in optometry. I had raised James and his twin brother, Clint, to make use of the natural bounty around them. It didn't take James long to discover the wealth of berries that thrived near his new home in the Pacific Northwest. Soon, I was receiving glowing letters and phone calls telling me about the numerous wild berries that were an easy drive from Portland.

"Dad, you ought to see the abundance of blackberries, blueberries, and thimbleberries here," was a typical sentence of correspondence during the summer months. "You ought to write another book," James stated.

Well, I had just gotten into writing *The Great Lakes Berry Book* (my third berry book) and didn't feel like taking on another project at the moment, so I let the suggestion fall.

Since James was working on a master's degree in plant ecology (wetland restoration, to be exact), I thought that maybe he and I could collaborate and do a father/son book.

When my friend Dot Heggie and I finally journeyed to Oregon and Washington to sample the berries, we were escorted around Oregon not by James and Tonya (by now James was at Iowa State finishing his masters and Tonya was doing her internship in Colorado), but rather by a good friend and his wife, Dave Hughes and Masako Tani.

Dave and Masako knew much of the country in Oregon from a fishing standpoint—Dave is a renowned fly fisher and has written a large number of books on the subject, and Masako writes a column on the out-of-doors for a Japanese magazine. They certainly knew their home turf. Dot and I were treated to beautiful vistas, tempting looking trout streams and a host of berries.

After leaving Dave and Masako, we journeyed north to Port Hadlock, Washington, to meet with Pat and Larry Robinson. Pat had acquired the local title of "berry fairy" and it only took us fifteen minutes before we realized that the title was well deserved. Pat and Larry knew every inch of the country within two hundred miles of Port Hadlock. They knew where the salmon berries, evergreen blackberries, and red huckleberries abounded. I photographed all that I could and marveled at how quickly Pat could pick. I thought I was quick, but she made me look like I had mittens on! Pat and Larry introduced us to berry patches that must have been made in heaven.

We left with deep regret, for our stay had been too short, but the memories of the great berry patches and wonderful people we visited buoyed us and made us realize that we had to return. We'll be back to the Pacific Northwest to renew our friendships, to go fishing, and to pick berries.

How to use this book:

We have designed this book so you can identify the common edible wild berries and fruits of the Pacific Northwest region, including northern California, Oregon, Washington, British Columbia, Idaho, and northern Nevada. We have tried to identify what the plants look like, their preferred habitat, when they flower, and when their fruits ripen.

We wrote the book for use by people of all levels of plant identification experience. We have tried to avoid terms not used in daily conversation, but in plant descriptions it is sometimes impossible to completely avoid botanical terms. Although you will find a complete glossary toward the end of the book, we will introduce the more commonly used terms here. When I mention berry, I am referring to any small, fleshy fruit. All berries are fruits and most berries are edible. A tree has only one stem and usually reaches a height greater than 20 feet. A shrub has multiple stems and usually reaches a height of less than 20 feet.

Your berry picking will benefit from preseason scouting. That way, you will have patches in mind when you go berry picking and, as a plus, you will spend more time out-of-doors. With the increased time outside comes a greater realization of the beauty and complexity of the living world about you. Berry picking is a good excuse to sample the out-of-doors and the bounty of this earth, but there are other things you can do in conjunction with berry picking: fishing, hiking, hunting, bird watching, and wildlife and wildflower photography to name a few.

We hope that you'll enjoy the book that James and I have put together for you. We hope that you are able to get out and enjoy the wealth of wild berries that abound in the Pacific Northwest and that you will come to realize that berry picking is a fun and tasty way to spend a day or a week. Happy picking!

HAZARDS

While berry picking can be a delightful way to spend a day, there are things that can turn your berry-picking expedition into a disaster.

One hazard can be poisonous berries. Your first rule in berry picking should be a simple one: if you have questions about a berry, **don't eat it!**

We have tried to thoroughly describe the common wild berries and fruits by text and photos; make sure you read the identification information and study the photos. If you still aren't sure, don't pick the berry. There are plenty of field guides on the market. Consult another one, or get an expert berry picker to help you identify the edible berries.

There really aren't many poisonous berries that can be confused with edible ones, but there are some. Several of the red berries—woody nightshade, baneberry, yew, and holly—can cause you a lot of grief.

Woody nightshade *(Solanum dulcamara)* prefers moist areas. You can find it growing along streams, springs, seeps, and standing water. It has purple, star-shaped flowers. The fruits ripen into red, elliptical-shaped berries that look a lot like miniature Italian tomatoes. The chemical compound in nightshade is solanine, a glycoalkaloid that produces two types of poisoning: irritant and nervous. Woody nightshade is a member of the same family that includes potatoes and tomatoes but with a crucial difference: it can kill you.

Baneberry (*Actaea rubra*) is a herbaceous perennial that grows in moist areas, shady forests, along stream banks and clearings. The light green leaves are highly divided. The berries are a bright, glossy red (a minority of the plants have glossy white berries) and look as though they were painted china—hence another name, chinaberry. The berries occur in vertical clusters of 10 to 20. The poison in baneberry is a glycoside: it can cause quickening of the heartbeat, gastroenteritis, dizziness, diarrhea, and vomiting. Fatalities have been reported.

A small evergreen tree or large shrub called a yew has dark green half-inch-long, pointed, flattened needles with a light, olive green underside; it almost looks like a spruce or fir. The western yew (*Taxus brevifolia*) has a berry-like fruit, summer into fall, that is red and very attractive. The "berry" looks somewhat like a red huckleberry but has a hole in the end. If you look in the hole, you can see the seed. While the jury is out on how poisonous it is, you had better leave it alone, for other species of yew are highly poisonous. Yew "berries" contain taxine, a complex alkaloid that is rapidly absorbed from the digestive tract and interferes with heart action. Case studies on humans have shown that alkaloids are strongly diuretic and cause severe ventricular rhythms. Initial symptoms include dizziness, dry throat, nausea, abdominal pain, and vomiting. It is for sure that the very common introduced species, Japanese yew (*Taxus japonicus*), a common ornamental landscaping shrub, and English yew (*Taxus baccata*) are poisonous and can be found wild throughout the Northwest.

Most of us have seen holly in Christmas wreaths. It has leathery, spiny green leaves with bright red berries. Holly (*Ilex opaca*) has escaped cultivation and is doing well in moist areas of Washington, Oregon, and British Columbia. Though birds can eat holly berries with impunity, humans are not so fortunate. The ripe berries are poisonous due to the chemical ilicin, which causes vomiting, diarrhea, and possible death if a person eats a large number of the berries.

It should be pointed out that chokecherry and bitter cherry have leaves, seeds, and twigs that contain two toxic chemicals: amygdalin and prunasin. Probably the biggest threat to humans is consuming the raw pit, rather than discarding the pit or cooking the cherry first. (Cooking breaks down the chemicals into harmless compounds.) According to an Internet report of the Canadian Agriculture Research Board on Poisonous Plants, compiled by Derek Munro, "Ingesting large quantities of red chokecherry fruits, without removing the seeds, has caused illness and death in children. The onset of symptoms is usually sudden and includes abdominal pain, vomiting, convulsions, inability to speak, labored breathing, coma, and death from asphyxiation." I want to emphasize that the chokecherry *pit* is what you should avoid swallowing. The pulp is edible whether it is cooked or raw. I doubt that you would bother eating the leaves or stems.

Remember that the seeds of crab apples, haws, and plums contain the same types of compounds as chokecherry pits. Cooking does break down the chemicals. Don't eat the raw seeds and you will be okay.

Two other plant species need mentioning. Though they won't kill you, they can make you miserable. These two plants are poison ivy and poison oak. Both belong to the genus *Toxicodendron* (formerly *Rhus)* and both have an oil, urushiol, in the plant parts such as leaves, stems, roots, and seeds. Contact with urushiol is known to cause blisters and severe dermatitis. If a person inhales smoke from burning poison ivy or poison oak or eats the berries, inflammation of the nasal passages, mouth, and throat can occur.

I can speak from experience that poison ivy and its cousins are to be left alone. The skin rashes that I have gotten from poison ivy are oozing, constantly itching, and have driven me to distraction. My first bad case of poison ivy came at the ripe age of seven. I was downwind of a fence row that my Dad was burning and I got in the smoke. Unfortunately, there was a lot of poison ivy in the fence row and I got it so bad that my eyes nearly swelled shut. Up until that time I had been deathly afraid of hypodermic needles, but when our family doctor told me I would feel better if I took the cortisone shot, I readily agreed. I can truthfully say that I'll take a hypodermic needle an eighth of an inch in diameter over a general poison ivy infection any day.

Poison ivy *(Toxicodendron rydbergii)* is a vine or small shrub with glossy compound leaves. The leaves are composed of three leaflets, each pointed at the tip, broadest near the base, and entire, or with a few large teeth. In autumn, the leaves turn hot orange or red before they fall. Poison ivy has white berries the size of BBs, in clusters of 10 to 20. Poison ivy occurs primarily east of the Cascades all the way to the East Coast.

Poison oak, *Toxicodendron diversilobum*, has compound leaves composed of 3 to 5 leaflets that have irregular, rounded lobes. The leaves are similar to those of white oak and turn bright red in autumn. Poison oak is more common in California where it occurs as a shrub 3 to 6 feet tall, but it is also found in the Cascade and Coastal ranges into Washington. It may occur in moister areas as a vine up to 50 feet long. Poison oak has white berries the size of split peas that occur in clusters of 3 to 10.

Perhaps it should be pointed out here that there are **no edible white berries,** since not only poison ivy, poison oak, and snowberry fall into this category, but white baneberry as well.

Other hazards fall under the animal category. Blueberries and huckleberries in particular are highly preferred bear food. While most of the Northwest is black bear country, you don't have to go far into British Columbia before grizzly bears are common. Regardless of the species, a human is no match for a bear; give them the patch and go find another. If you are picking in an area with lots of bears or an area that has a history of bear attacks, carry a large can of pepper spray: it is a potent bear repellant.

Pat Robinson, my good friend and world-class berry picker, contends that her biggest fear is of insects like yellow jackets, wasps, and bees. She says, "I fear stepping into a bee or yellow jacket nest. The insects could sting me so many times that I might have a rough time recovering." Suffice it to say, watch out for stinging insects!

In the eastern part of the Northwest, rattlesnakes are common. A snakebite is a serious injury. If you should be bitten by a rattlesnake, stay calm, and get to a hospital as soon as possible for antivenin shots.

Most all of the berries that are listed in this book are pioneer species, that is, they occur in disturbed areas. In the Northwest, that means logged areas. Unfortunately, that also means herbicides. Most of the lumber companies use herbicides to suppress growth of trees and shrubs that they don't want growing. In other words, if you see wilted, brown, unhealthy looking shrubs, don't pick the berries.

This same scenario holds for road and power line right-of-ways. I saw highways in Washington where the scenic view sites had been sprayed to give people an unimpeded view of a lake or mountain. Remember: If the plant doesn't look healthy, don't pick the berries!

I'll close this chapter with a paragraph taken from Mount Hood National Forest's pamphlet, *Huckleberry Time*: "It is easy to lose your way in the enthusiasm of picking. Go in small groups, orienting yourselves from time to time. Keep your eye on the sun, protect your skin from overexposure and return to your car before dark."

Blackberry

Blackberries have long been a favorite of mine. Some of my earliest recollections of berry picking involve reaching through briars to pick those juicy, drooping, glossy black, thimble-shaped berries. My, how sweet they tasted to me. So many thoughts run through my mind when I think of eating blackberries: their luscious taste in pie and jam, and a bowl full of them covered with milk and sprinkled with sugar. All these thoughts get my salivary glands running in torrents.

I was dumbfounded by the widespread distribution of blackberries in the Pacific Northwest. It seems everywhere we traveled in Oregon and Washington, blackberries lined the borrow pits and fallow fields. From all that I could ascertain, blackberries had gone from a welcome plant to a noxious plant in a hurry. Incidentally, the only other place that I have seen blackberries growing so prolifically was New Zealand; blackberries are classified as a noxious weed there, too.

Noxious weed or not, blackberries taste great and are fun to pick. Any time a person can pick a gallon or two of big, tasty berries in less than an hour, I would say that person was doing all right. With blackberries in the

Northwest, I would hazard a guess that most berry pickers should be able to pick two gallons an hour when the blackberries are at the peak of ripeness.

When Dave Hughes and his wife, Masako Tani, showed Dot and me a small patch of blackberries on the east side of Portland, I thought I had died and gone to heaven. Though the patch was less than an acre, there must have been 20 gallons of blackberries hanging there inviting us to pick them. I had a photography schedule that demanded that I photograph as many species of berries in four days as possible; berry picking conflicted with the schedule. Fortunately, Dot and Masako picked while I photographed the more tempting clusters of berries.

After I had taken a couple dozen different photos of the blackberries, I couldn't stand it any longer. I grabbed a bucket and started picking. Dave reminded me that we had to move on, so I said, "Just give me 15 minutes and then I'll be ready to go." The berries were so plentiful that I managed to nearly fill the gallon bucket before the 15 minutes expired. I probably would have had a gallon if my hand hadn't gotten lost between the bush and the bucket and somehow ended up at my mouth! When we left that spot, I had purple hands, scratched arms, and enough photos to satisfy my book needs. Since we had four more days of traveling, Dot and I gave our take to Dave and Masako.

Two days later, Pat and Larry Robinson showed us a blackberry patch at a roadside park in northern Washington that definitely qualified as a trophy berry patch. We had about one hour before dark. Our time was limited, but suffice it to say that we managed to pick a passel. I remember stepping on the blackberry canes to work my way into the center of the patch. Each step involved thorns sticking me in the calves and thighs, but it also revealed a half dozen succulent clusters of perfectly ripened blackberries. The berries fell into my hand when I touched them. Many were too soft to put in the bucket, so unfortunately I had to eat them.

I was working on topping off my second gallon when Pat said we'd better quit. It was then that I realized I had been picking by feel for the past 15 minutes. We ended up with 7 gallons from that sweet spot. It had to have been the best blackberry patch I had ever had the privilege to pick.

IDENTIFICATION

There are several species of blackberries that occur in the Pacific Northwest. Only one, however, is native; the rest have been introduced. The five-petaled, white flowers are arranged in raceme-like clusters, with 6 to 15 flowers per cluster. They typically blossom in May.

Perhaps the most common is the Himalayan blackberry, *Rubus discolor*. This introduced species seems to have taken over most of the Northwest. It has a palmately compound leaf with 3 to 5 leaflets. The leaflets are oval-shaped with serrated margins. Of course the reddish-hued canes have curved, hefty prickles about $1/4$ inch long. Himalayan blackberries can be found from sea level up to mid-mountain level in waste areas, recently disturbed areas, and roadsides. They ripen in clusters of 10 to 20 from mid-August into September. Usually about a third or so will be ripe at a time. If the blackberry plants have plenty of moisture, the berries are about thimble size. The ripening berries turn from light green to bright red to glossy black.

Another introduced species goes by two common names: cut-leaf blackberry or evergreen blackberry. Its scientific name is *Rubus laciniatus*. The plant gets its name from the deeply incised leaflets—so much so that the leaflets often appear to be double-pinnately compound. The alternately arranged leaves have from 3 to 5 leaflets that stay green all year long. The distribution is similar to the Himalayan blackberry. The berries ripen from mid-August into mid-September. The clusters contain 10 to 20 berries, usually with only a third ripe at one time.

There are those who will contend that the blackberry commonly known as trailing blackberry or dewberry (*R. ursinus*) is the best tasting of all the Northwest blackberries. Trailing blackberry is perhaps the best common name for this species because the plant can grow up to 20 feet long, but doesn't attain much altitude as it trails over rocks and logs. The plant is an invader that quickly takes over disturbed areas—in the Northwest that means logged areas. You can find plenty of trailing blackberries two years after an area has been logged. This species ripens earlier than the two introduced species—look for it July into mid-August.

The pinnately compound leaves have 3 to 5 leaflets that have serrated margins. The leaves are arranged alternately. The prickles aren't as pronounced as with the introduced species, but still they can tear a hole in your hide if you get in a hurry to pick this native berry.

RECIPES

Blackberry Liqueur

2 quarts gin
2 quarts blackberries
6 cups sugar

Put all ingredients in a gallon container. Shake once a day, everyday, for 3 weeks. Strain through a cheesecloth or a coffee filter, and bottle.

Pat Robinson, Port Hadlock, Washington

Blackberry Cordial

1 quart vodka
2 quarts blackberries
4 cups sugar

Place all ingredients in a gallon jar, covered. Stir every few days. Let brew 2 months or more. Strain through a cheesecloth or a coffee filter, then bottle.

Pat Robinson, Port Hadlock, Washington

Blackberry Dumplings

flour
baking powder
milk
berries
sugar

Dumplings:

For every cup of flour, use 1 teaspoon baking powder. Add enough milk to make a gooey, spoonable mixture. Drop by spoonfuls into the base.

Base:

Fill the bottom of a cast-iron skillet with a full layer of berries. Add sugar to taste. Let mixture simmer to cook berries. Drop spoonfuls of dumpling batter into the berry mixture. Simmer over burner, covered, for 20 minutes, then flip dumplings and finish cooking for 5 to 10 more minutes, covered.

Blackberry Cake

1 1/2 cups sugar
1 cup butter
3 eggs
1 teaspoon baking soda
1/2 cup sour milk
3 cups flour
1 teaspoon baking powder
1/2 teaspoon salt
1 teaspoon cinnamon
1 teaspoon cloves
1 teaspoon allspice
2 cups blackberries*

Cream sugar and butter. Add eggs. Dissolve soda in sour milk. Sift dry ingredients together and add alternately with milk and soda mixture to creamed sugar and butter. Fold in blackberries.

(continued on next page)

Bake at 350 degrees for 30 to 40 minutes or until done.

*Black raspberries, raspberries, salmonberries, strawberries, and thimbleberries may be substituted.

Pat Robinson, Port Hadlock, Washington

Blackberry Pie

Standard pie crust (see pie crust recipe on page 124)
1 quart blackberries (trailing blackberries preferred)
$2^1/_2$ tablespoons tapioca
1 cup sugar (more if you have a sweet tooth)

Roll out pie crust. Place crust in pan. Mix berries, tapioca, and sugar; place in pie shell, then cover with top pie crust. Place pie on a cookie sheet (to prevent overflowing onto bottom of oven). Bake at 400 degrees for 20 minutes, then reduce heat to 350 and bake for an additional 40 minutes.

Hope Hughes, Astoria, Oregon

Blackberry Slump

1 quart trailing blackberries*
1 cup sugar
1 tablespoon tapioca
1 to 2 cups biscuit mix, sweetened slightly (1 tablespoon
   sugar per cup is a good rule of thumb)
1 egg
$^1/_2$ to $^2/_3$ cup milk

Combine berries, sugar, and tapioca. Heat on stovetop until tapioca clarifies. Combine biscuit mix, egg, and milk to form a dumpling mixture; spoon in dumplings. Let dumplings bubble over burner for 20 minutes with tight lid.

*Other blackberries may be used as well as black raspberries, thimbleberries, raspberries, and strawberries.

Hope Hughes, Astoria, Oregon

Blackberry Jelly

3 cups juice from Himalayan blackberries (from approximately
   2 quarts of blackberries)
$1/4$ cup lemon juice
I package MCP pectin
3 cups sugar*
$1/4$ teaspoon butter or margarine to reduce foaming

Combine berry juice, lemon juice, and pectin; stir thoroughly. Bring to full boil, stirring almost constantly. Stir in sugar and return to full boil for 2 minutes. Add butter or margarine to reduce foaming. Skim off foam and pour immediately into sterilized jars. Attach lids and rings and place in a boiling water bath for 10 minutes.

*Note: This is a reduced-sugar variation of a pectin recipe that warns not to reduce the sugar. For me, it jells if the jelly is made in a pot big enough to allow it to boil vigorously. If it fails to jell, it makes an excellent syrup.

Dave Hughes, Portland, Oregon

Blackberry Juice Bars

Render the juice from I gallon of blackberries*. Sweeten to taste. Add water if the juice is too thick. (Usual mix is half juice and half water.) Freeze in juice bar containers available at your favorite store, or in ice cube trays.

*You can also use the juice from serviceberries, salal, salmonberries, and blueberries for this recipe.

Masako Tani, Portland, Oregon

Wild Blackberry and Peach Cobbler

1 cup all-purpose flour
$1/2$ cup granulated sugar
$1 1/2$ teaspoons baking powder
$1/2$ cup milk
$1/4$ cup butter or margarine, softened
$1/4$ cup packed brown sugar
1 tablespoon cornstarch
$1/2$ cup cold water
3 cups sliced fresh peaches
$1 1/4$ cups fresh blackberries*
1 tablespoon butter or margarine
1 tablespoon lemon juice
$1/4$ teaspoon ground nutmeg or cinnamon

For topping: Stir together flour, granulated sugar, and baking powder. Add milk and $1/4$ cup butter or margarine. Stir till smooth, set aside.

For filling: Stir together brown sugar and cornstarch in a medium saucepan; stir in water. Add peaches and blackberries. Cook and stir over medium heat till thickened and bubbly. Add 1 tablespoon each butter and lemon juice; stir till butter melts.

Pour into a $1 1/2$-quart ungreased casserole. Spoon topping over hot filling, spreading evenly. Sprinkle with a mixture of coarse sugar and nutmeg or cinnamon. Place on a shallow baking pan in oven.

Bake cobbler at 350 degrees for about 35 minutes or until bubbly and a toothpick inserted into crust comes out clean. Serve warm with ice cream, if desired.

Yield: 6 servings

*Blueberries, huckleberries, raspberries (red and black), strawberries, and thimbleberries can be used.

Gary Hinman, Angels Camp, California

Blackberry Syrup*

2 cups blackberry juice (from approximately 1 $^1/_2$ quarts blackberries)
2 cups sugar
2 cups white corn syrup

Measure juice into 6- or 8-quart pot. Heat juice to boiling; add sugar, stirring until dissolved. Add corn syrup, heat to boiling, and simmer about 5 minutes. Pour into hot, sterilized jars. Seal with lids and screw bands. Place in boiling water bath 10 minutes.

*This recipe can be used for just about all the berries in this book.

James Krumm, Casper, Wyoming

Blackcap Raspberry

Blackcap or black raspberry is a native species of the Pacific Northwest. Though not the same species of black raspberry that I knew in my home state of Michigan, it is close in both looks and taste.

Blackcaps are highly favored by birds as well as humans. Sometimes it is a race to see who gets to the ripe berries first. Thanks to the birds, however, blackcaps are widely distributed.

In my memory, blackcaps were the first berry I ever enjoyed picking. Maybe it was because my parents didn't grow black raspberries; they grew wild, and I could venture out alone to pick them. There was a little bit of pride involved in it, too. The neighbor boys thought they knew the surrounding woods and river floodplains pretty well. I thought I knew them better.

By the time I was in my early teens, I would slip away after doing my morning chores. With my berry bucket in hand, I would head downstream along the river. In less than 100 yards I would start finding large clumps of black raspberries in the moderately shaded second growth timber. Some of the blackcaps would be as big as rounded thimbles. The longer it took these secluded berries to ripen, the sweeter, juicier, and plumper they were. The big berries gave me a quick start on filling my bucket.

I would work my way farther downriver, going to every patch I knew of and checking likely looking spots for new patches. In a matter of one or two hours, I would have a full 2-gallon bucket of black raspberries. I would prance back home and present the full bucket to my mother. I had speculated all the way home what she might do with them. Usually, she would make a black raspberry pie; sometimes she would make jelly or jam. (I liked the jam better because of the chewy seeds.) The praise that my mother heaped on me was enough to make me want to go out and do it again two days later when the next batch of blackcaps would be ripe.

Somehow or another, Mom would let the neighbor ladies know that I had picked a big bucketful of berries. Sometimes it was as simple as giving the neighbors a jar of jelly or—horrors—a pie, but the word would get out and the other neighbor boys would be under the gun to equal my feat. Anyway, for a kid who couldn't compete too well in athletics, it was my way of being on the first team. Ah, so much for the competitive world of a teenage boy and the minor triumphs achieved with a full bucket of blackcaps.

IDENTIFICATION

Blackcap or black raspberry belongs to the family Rosaceae and the genus *Rubus*. All the raspberries, blackberries, salmonberries, and thimbleberries belong to the same family and genus. The species name for black raspberry is *leucodermis*, which means white-skin. The scientific name springs from the fact that black raspberry stems are covered with a whitish bloom.

The stems have curved, flattened prickles. Black raspberry grows as high as 6 feet, but often will bend down so that the tips of the branches touch the ground. Oftentimes the tips will root, forming another plant.

The alternately arranged leaves are light green in color on top and nearly white underneath. The leaf is composed of 3, or sometimes 5, leaflets that are rounded at the base and pointed at the tips. The leaflet margins are toothed.

Blackcaps blossom late May through June, depending on the elevation. The blossoms are white to pink in color and appear in clusters of 3 to 7 at the ends of the stems or in the axis of the leaf.

The berries ripen July into August. The berries turn from light green to bright red to glossy purple or black when ripe. The berries are slightly hairy, about $^3/_8$ inch in diameter, domed, and like a red raspberry—only black. When you pick a black raspberry or a red raspberry, the center (receptacle) stays on the stem, whereas when you pick a blackberry the center comes with the berry.

Black raspberries like moderate to full sunlight. You will find blackcaps growing in disturbed sites such as clearcuts, burned clearcuts, along logging roads, open forests, and thickets. They range from sea level to midway in the mountains from British Columbia south to southern California and as far east as Montana and Utah.

Most of the time black raspberry is fairly abundant, but it might take some searching before you find a substantial patch. If you find such a patch, you should be able to pick a gallon. I would say that in three out of four years, you should be able to pick a gallon of black raspberries at the height of the season.

RECIPES

Black Raspberry Jelly

3 quarts black raspberries
1 cup water
$^1/_4$ cup lemon juice

In a large (6- or 8-quart) pan or pot, crush the black raspberries, add water and lemon juice, and place over high heat. Bring to a full, rolling boil. Strain and reserve juice.

3³/₄ cups black raspberry juice
1 package powdered pectin
5¹/₂ cups sugar

Place juice back in pot. Add powdered pectin and stir until dissolved. Place over high heat and bring to a full, rolling boil, stirring constantly. Add sugar and continue to stir constantly. Bring to a full, rolling boil, and boil for 1 minute. Remove from heat, skim foam if necessary, pour hot jelly into sterilized jars, place on lids, secure with screw bands and place in a boiling water bath for 10 minutes.

Yield: six 8-ounce jars.

Dot Heggie, Gillette, Wyoming

Black Raspberry Pie

1 quart black raspberries
1 cup sugar
3 tablespoons flour
dash of salt
3 pats of butter
1 unbaked pie shell and top crust (see pie crust recipe on page 124)

Combine black raspberries, sugar, flour, and salt. Place in pie shell. Dot with butter. Cover with top pie crust. Pierce the crust with a fork in four or five places. Bake at 450 degrees for 10 minutes, then lower temperature to 350 and bake for 30 more minutes.

Emily Krumm, Eaton Rapids, Michigan

Hobo Cookies

4 cups flour
1 cup shortening
1 cup butter (or margarine)
1 cup milk
1 cake yeast or 1 tablespoon dry yeast
1 teaspoon vanilla
$1/2$ teaspoon salt
3 egg yolks, lightly beaten
1 8-ounce jar black raspberry jelly or jam*

Preheat oven to 350 degrees. Combine flour, shortening, and butter; work together like pie dough. Set aside. Scald milk, cool to lukewarm, dissolve yeast in it, and let rest 10 to 15 minutes. Add vanilla, salt, and egg yolks. Mix thoroughly.

Mix the yeast mixture into the flour mixture. Put sugar on a board as you would flour to roll out pie dough. Roll dough $1/4$- to $1/8$-inch thick. Cut into 2-inch squares. Add a heaping teaspoon of jelly or jam to the center of the square. Pinch the corners of the square together. Bake on greased baking sheets 12 to 15 minutes, or until dough just starts to brown on the edges.

*Any of the jams and jellies listed in the book would work for this recipe. Try a variety of them.

Emily Krumm, Eaton Rapids, Michigan

"I have to admit, this cookie recipe is still my favorite after all these years." Bob Krumm

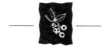

Blueberry and Huckleberry

While a number of Northwest berry pickers refer to most of this group as "huckleberries," all belong to the genus, Vaccinium, the blueberry genus. True huckleberries are an Eastern genus, Gaylusaccia. Oh well, the upshot of the whole deal is that regardless of what they are called, they taste great! Huckleberries and blueberries are favorites among berry pickers all across the United States. There are blueberry and huckleberry festivals from Maine to Oregon.

We had a wonderful time picking red huckleberries with Dave and Masako in the Coastal Range west of Portland. It was quite an expedition with Dot, Dave, Masako, and their daughter, Kosumo, who happily rode in the kiddie pack as Dave hiked into the forest along his favorite creek.

Masako loves to pick berries, and it didn't take long for her to proclaim that she had found red huckleberries. I looked about and didn't see any berry bushes in the understory of the forest, but then I spotted Masako on top of a gigantic stump eagerly picking the largesse she had found there. I soon discovered that red huckleberry (*V. parvifolium*) frequently grow on tree stumps. (I later found out that the growth habit was the result of birds depositing the seeds on the stumps.)

Masako is quite petite, and to see her on top of an 8-foot-high stump that was probably 10 feet in diameter gave me a perspective on how big the tree must have been. The 8-foot-tall red huckleberry bush didn't stand a chance; the willowy branches yielded to Masako's insistent pulling and tugging. She clambered up the stump, pulled on the branches to bend it over, and quickly picked the heavily laden bush. Masako picked 2 quarts of huckleberries before the area was picked out.

That day was one of the most fun berry-picking expeditions I had ever been on, but to my surprise, the following day was just as much fun, if not more. We drove east of Portland into Mount Hood National Forest. On a whim, I asked Dave to drive down an inviting side road. Within 200 yards of the main road, I was spotting red elderberry, blueberries, and salmonberries. When Dave finally parked the car at a pullout, it was as though we had stepped into berry-picker paradise.

Wherever I looked from the car, I could see blueberry bushes laden with deep purple berries. Scattered among them were bushes loaded with powder-blue blueberries. It took me about two minutes to discover that there were several patches of wild strawberry within 50 yards of the car; all the patches were loaded with scrumptious berries. Farther along the road was a bumper crop of yellow salmonberries with a scattering of red ones.

Masako was off and picking as were Dot and Dave. I had photography chores to accomplish. It was agonizing for me to find laden berry bushes and do nothing more than photograph them, but I finally got all my photos and then I jumped into picking.

By that time, we only had an hour before we had to head back to Portland so we could pick up Kosumo at preschool. I managed to pick a couple of quarts of blueberries before Dave announced it was time to leave. Masako didn't want to quit the productive patch she had found. Finally, Dave had to take Masako's overflowing berry bucket to get her to come in—and then she only returned when she had filled her hands full of blueberries.

ॐ

IDENTIFICATION

Blueberries and huckleberries belong to the family Ericaceae. There are at least eight species in the Northwest that can be called "blueberries" or "huckleberries." The species range in height from a few inches to 10 feet high and inhabit areas as diverse as bogs to subalpine tundra to coniferous forests.

Some of the more important species are *Vaccinium ovalifolium* (oval-leafed blueberry), *V. membranaceum* (black huckleberry), *V. parvifolium* (red huckleberry), *V. ovatum* (evergreen huckleberry), *V. uliginosum* (bog blueberry), *V. caespitosum* (dwarf bilberry or blueberry), and *V. alaskaense* (Alaska blueberry).

The color of the flower ranges from bronze to pinkish to white and variations in between. The petals are fused to form a bell- or urn-shaped flower. Most of the species have deciduous leaves, while one has evergreen leaves. All species have alternate arrangement of leaves. The leaves of all the species are simple with no lobes—most have entire margins—and some have fine serrations and vary from a light, bright green to a medium green. Leaves often develop a reddish tint or have darker spots on them. The evergreen huckleberry has thicker, leathery leaves with small, sharp teeth. It retains its leaves year round.

One distinguishing feature of the genus is that the twigs are quite fine. The twigs of most of the species are strongly to slightly angled in cross-section (not round), with protruding corners, or "wings," running lengthwise. Evergreen huckleberry, dwarf blueberry, and bog blueberry lack this trait. The young twigs of the red huckleberry are bright green all year. With a little practice, you'll find it easy to identify patches of blueberries, even in the winter, by noting their unique twigs and the characteristic leaves (when present).

The berries range in color from bright red (red huckleberry), to powder blue (such as oval-leaved blueberry), to blue-black and purple (such as evergreen, black, and Alaska blueberries). The berry size ranges from slightly less than pea-sized to almost twice pea-sized (if you're lucky). The berries have a circular scar, or flat spot, on them opposite the stem, from where the petals were attached. Sometimes the remains of the petals can still be seen, and on some it almost resembles a small bull's-eye. The berries will ripen anytime between late July and October. All taste delicious, but the flavor varies between species.

RECIPES

Red Huckleberry Jelly

2¹/₂ cups sugar, divided*
1 package pectin for lower sugar
5 cups red huckleberry juice (from approximately 3¹/₂ quarts red huckleberries)
¹/₂ teaspoon margarine or butter

Mix ¹/₄ cup sugar and pectin in small bowl.

Place juice in a large pot, and stir pectin-sugar mix into juice. Add margarine or butter. Bring to a full boil, stirring constantly. Stir in remaining sugar. Bring to a full, rolling boil, and boil for 1 minute, stirring constantly. Remove from heat, skim off foam, and pour immediately into hot, sterilized jars. Attach lids and rings, and place in boiling water bath 10 minutes.

*Note: This is a reduced sugar variation of a recipe that is already reduced. If cooked well, it should jell, as it has for us.

Masako Tani, Portland, Oregon

Red Huckleberry Jelly

2 quarts red huckleberries
1 tablespoon lemon juice
3 cups sugar

Place berries in a heavy pot with a little water. Boil for 10 minutes. Squeeze through a jelly bag. Strain through a clean bag a second time, but do not squeeze the second time. Put both juices—huckleberry and lemon—back in pot and boil for 5 minutes. Add sugar and boil rapidly until the mixture tests for jelling (see sheet test on page 130). Remove from heat and skim off foam. Pour into sterilized jars, place on lids, adjust screw bands tightly and place in a boiling water bath for 10 minutes.

Pat Robinson, Port Hadlock, Washington

Huckleberry Jam

6 cups crushed huckleberries* (from approximately 2 quarts
  huckleberries)
1 package powdered pectin
8 cups sugar

Prepare 9 half-pint jars. Wash and drain berries. Crush. Put 6 cups fruit into a 6-quart pan. Stir in pectin and bring to a boil, stirring constantly. Add sugar, stirring constantly. Bring to a full, rolling boil; boil for 2 minutes. Remove from heat and skim. Place in jars and attach lids and screw bands. Process in a boiling water bath for 10 minutes.

*Use half huckleberries and half salal berries for a less sweet jam.

From *Huckleberry Time*, Mount Hood National Forest, 2955 N.W. Division St., Gresham, Oregon 97030. (This is a handy booklet, which has maps of some of the better huckleberry spots in the Mount Hood National Forest.)

Huckleberry Muffins

I cup quick oats
I cup sour milk
I cup flour
I teaspoon baking powder
$1/2$ teaspoon baking soda
I teaspoon salt
$3/4$ cup brown sugar
I egg, beaten
$1/4$ cup melted butter
I cup huckleberries*

Preheat oven to 400 degrees. Combine oats and sour milk and let stand. Combine all dry ingredients. Add egg and melted butter to oats; mix well. Add dry ingredients and stir only until moistened. Fold in huckleberries. Fill muffin cups $3/4$ full. Bake for 15 to 20 minutes.

*Raspberry (red), strawberry, and thimbleberry may be substituted.

From *Huckleberry Time*

Cracker Pie

$1 1/4$ cup sugar, divided
3 egg whites
$1/2$ teaspoon baking powder
$2/3$ cup coarsely chopped nuts
16 soda crackers, broken up, but not fine
I teaspoon vanilla
I cup huckleberries
whipped cream

Preheat oven to 300 degrees. Add 1 cup sugar slowly to egg whites and beat until stiff. Fold in baking powder, nuts, soda crackers, and vanilla. Bake for 30 minutes. Sweeten huckleberries with remaining sugar. Spread evenly over the pie, then top with whipped cream.

Marty Corbett, Spokane, Washington

Huckleberry Cheesecake

Crust:

- 1 cup graham cracker crumbs
- 1 cup flour
- $^3/_4$ cup butter
- 1 cup finely chopped nuts

Combine all crust ingredients and bake in a 9 x 13-inch pan for 10 minutes at 350 degrees. Cool.

Filling:

- 1 8-ounce package cream cheese
- 1 cup powdered sugar
- 2 cups whipped cream

Combine cream cheese with powdered sugar. Fold in whipped cream. No baking required.

Topping:

- 4 cups huckleberries
- $^3/_4$ cup water
- 4 tablespoons cornstarch
- 1 cup sugar
- 1 tablespoon lemon juice
- 1 tablespoon butter

Simmer 1 heaping cup of huckleberries with water for 3 or 4 minutes. Mix cornstarch and sugar and add to mixture. Cook and stir until thick. Add lemon juice and butter and cool slightly. Add rest of huckleberries. Stir lightly and pour on top.

Marty Corbett, Spokane, Washington

Huckleberry Cake

2 cups flour
1 teaspoon soda
$^1/_2$ teaspoon salt
1 egg
1 teaspoon vanilla
$^1/_2$ cup butter
1 cup sour milk
1$^1/_2$ cups brown sugar
1$^1/_2$ cups huckleberries

Sift together flour, soda, and salt. Add egg, vanilla, butter, sour milk, and brown sugar. Mix for 4 to 5 minutes. Stir in huckleberries. Put in greased 13 x 9 x 2-inch pan and top with the following mixture:

$^1/_2$ cup brown sugar
$^1/_4$ cup white sugar
1 tablespoon melted butter
$^1/_2$ cup nuts
1 teaspoon cinnamon

Bake at 350 degrees for 40 to 50 minutes.

Pat Robinson, Port Hadlock, Washington

Trail Jam

1 cup tart berries (blueberries or huckleberries*)
$^2/_3$ cup sugar
1 tablespoon lemon juice
1 whole cinnamon stick (optional)

To make fresh berry jam while camping:

In a pan combine berries, sugar, lemon juice, and cinnamon stick. Over a brisk fire, boil mixture, stirring until it reaches desired thickness. Serve warm or cooled. Makes 1$^1/_4$ cups to put on pancakes or spread on campfire biscuits.

*Gooseberries, strawberries, thimbleberries, and raspberries can also be used.

From *Huckleberry Time*

Huckleberry Crepes

1 cup sifted flour
2 tablespoons sugar
4 eggs
1 cup milk
1 cup water
sugared huckleberries

Sift flour with sugar. With a hand whisk, whisk eggs; add flour mixture and beat until smooth.

Add milk and water. Stir into batter until smooth. Let batter stand for at least 30 minutes.

Heat a lightly oiled heavy skillet. Drop 1 tablespoon batter onto center of skillet, shifting skillet to allow batter to spread out into a thin layer, and cook 1 or 2 minutes. Turn the crepe over. Slide onto rack and keep warm with other cooked crepes stacked on top of one another. Fill the crepes with sugared huckleberries.

Yield: approximately 15 to 20 crepes.

Alma Snell, Fort Smith, Montana

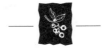

Chokecherry and Bitter Cherry

Both bitter cherry and chokecherry are not high on my list of those berries that I pick to eat as is. These cherries will make you pucker up and roll your lips up — they taste as though they are composed entirely of alum. Since bitter cherries can be used interchangeably with chokecherries, I'll merely write about my experiences with chokecherries.

As I mentioned in the introduction, there were berries that my mother didn't bother with, and chokecherry was one of them. She had plenty of pie cherries and sweet black cherries; why should she waste her time on such a vile tasting cherry?

It took me a year or two in Wyoming before I found out why people bother with it. In the first place, chokecherry is widespread and, secondly, it bears abundant fruit. The third and most compelling reason is that there is a wide variety of delectable treats that can be prepared from chokecherry. The list ranges from jelly to syrup to pies to cordials to pemmican, with lots of pleasant surprises along the way.

My twin sons, James and Clint, used to be reluctant to pick chokecherries but craved chokecherry jelly and syrup. It seemed like they just wouldn't pick any berries with me when they were around the ripe old age of ten, so I didn't push them. When they called in the middle of the winter asking for jelly, I simply replied that since they didn't pick any chokecherries, I didn't make any jelly. It was amazing the next time they visited me, I not only didn't have to prod them, but they picked a 5-gallon bucket full without my saying one word. The full bucket was strategically located on the kitchen table when I arrived home from work.

Actually, I think that the boys now prefer to pick chokecherries over about any other type. The reasons are relatively simple: chokecherries are easy to find since they are widespread, they don't have any thorns or prickles, and most importantly, the large pea-sized cherries occur in convenient clumps (racemes) of 8 to 20. A picker can pull a handful of chokecherries with each grasp if it's a good bush. At that rate, it will only take an hour or so to pick 2 to 3 gallons. By the way, since most recipes call for just the juice from chokecherries, you'll need at least a gallon of them to make a simple recipe such as jelly. Your chances of getting that many are excellent, however.

My friends Dwight and Jamie Hurich like to plan a weekend fishing trip around chokecherry season. They select a stream that they know will have good fishing and groves of chokecherries. Though both love to fish, they also enjoy picking chokecherries for use as syrup, jelly, and, their favorite, wine.

꩜

IDENTIFICATION

Chokecherry (*Prunus virginiana*) and bitter cherry (*P. emarginata*) are members of the rose family. Chokecherry has a much more widespread distribution, however, for you will find it across the continental United States and from the Arctic Circle to Mexico. While chokecherry prefers moderate amounts of moisture, it will make do in a desert with just a seep to give it sustenance.

Both bitter cherry and chokecherry are pioneer species. You will find them along the edges of woods, burns, abandoned farmlands, and timber cuts where they can get plenty of sun. Both usually grow in groves of 10 to 50. Chokecherry might reach 25 feet in height, but 8 to 12 feet is more common. The bitter cherry I observed in Oregon and Washington seemed to grow taller than chokecherry. Look for bitter cherry to reach heights of 35 to 60 feet, with 15 to 20 feet common.

Both chokecherry and bitter cherry have brown bark with prominent lenticels (breathing pores). Both have simple leaves that are arranged alternately, but chokecherry has a more pointed leaf tip (more lanceolate) than does bitter cherry. Chokecherry leaves are also deeper green in color. Both species have leaves with serrated edges.

Bitter cherry blossoms in late April into May, depending on the elevation, while chokecherry blossoms early to mid-May. Chokecherry has small, creamy white, 5-petaled flowers that occur in elongated clusters called racemes. Bitter cherry also has creamy white, 5-petaled flowers, but in a looser flower cluster.

Both ripen in late July through August and on into September, depending on elevation. Chokecherries turn from green to wine red to glossy black when ripening. Bitter cherries turn from green to bright red. Both cherries have a large pit and are only pea-sized to maybe $1^1/_2$ times pea size. They have a bitter taste that must be tempered greatly with sugar. Both make excellent jellies, syrups, and wines.

RECIPES

Remember that you can use chokecherry and bitter cherry interchangeably, or mix them.

Chokecherry Jelly

3$^1/_2$ cups chokecherry juice (from approximately 2 quarts chokecherries)
1 box pectin
4$^1/_2$ cups sugar

Stir pectin into chokecherry juice. After brought to a full, rolling boil, stir in sugar. Bring to another full, rolling boil while stirring constantly. Boil for 1 minute. Remove from heat, skim foam if necessary. Pour into prepared, sterilized jars. Place lids and rings on jars. Process in boiling water bath for 5 minutes.

Milly Mathiasson, Lewistown, Montana

Chokecherry Syrup

3 cups chokecherry juice (from approximately 2 quarts chokecherries)
1 cup white corn syrup
2 cups sugar

Boil all ingredients together 10 minutes. Put in hot, sterilized jars. Seal and process 8 minutes in boiling water bath.

Montana State University-Yellowstone County Extension Service

Chokecherry Daiquiri

For the chokecherry syrup:

4 cups fresh chokecherry juice (from approximately 3 quarts
  chokecherries)
4 cups sugar

For the daiquiris:

$1/_2$ cup chokecherry syrup
$3/_4$ cup sweet-and-sour bar concentrate
1 cup rum
about 3 cups ice cubes or crushed ice

Combine the chokecherry juice and sugar in a large saucepan and bring to a rolling boil over high heat. (At this point, you may want to can the syrup, using traditional canning procedures. In that way, it will keep for a year or more on your pantry shelf.) Chill the syrup in the refrigerator prior to mixing the daiquiris, or it will not make the "slush" type drink this is supposed to be. Then combine all the ingredients for the daiquiri in a blender. Blend on high speed for about 30 seconds, or until the ice is incorporated into the cocktail. Pour into suitable glasses, and garnish with either a spiral of fresh lime or a sprig of fresh mint. Serve.

Yield: 8 servings.

Storage: Store the blended daiquiris in a covered plastic container in the freezer for up to a week.

Nancy and Dave Brannon, Cody, Wyoming
Feasting in the Forest

Chokecherry Wine

2$\frac{1}{2}$ pounds fully ripe chokecherries
1 cup red grape concentrate or 1 pound raisins
7 pints water
2$\frac{1}{4}$ pounds sugar
$\frac{1}{2}$ teaspoon acid blend*
$\frac{1}{2}$ teaspoon pectic enzyme*
1 teaspoon nutrient*
1 Campden, crushed*
1 package wine-making yeast*

*These ingredients can be found in any brewer's supply store. Ask someone at the store for advice on what type of wine-making yeast will work best for your recipe.

Wash and remove stems, leaves, and badly bruised fruit. Mash cherries without breaking the pits. Using nylon straining bag (the Hurichs use a panty hose leg), mash and squeeze out juice into primary fermentor (a 5-gallon, or larger, plastic garbage pail). Keeping all pulp in straining bag, tie top and place in primary. Stir in all other ingredients *except* yeast. Cover primary. After 24 hours, add yeast. Cover primary. Stir daily, check specific gravity with a wine-making hydrometer (available at brewer's supply store), and press pulp lightly to aid extraction. When ferment reaches specific gravity 1.030 (about 5 days), strain juice from bag. Syphon wine off sediment into secondary fermentor (a 5-gallon glass jug). Attach airlock (purchase at brewer's supply store). When ferment is complete (about 3 to 4 more weeks), syphon wine off sediment into another clean 5-gallon glass jug. Reattach airlock. Syphon wine again in 2 months and again, if necessary, before bottling.

Dwight & Jamie Hurich, Gillette, Wyoming.
Modified from *Wine Makers Recipe Handbook*
by Raymond Massaccesi, 1971.

Bitter Cherry/Apple Butter

4 cups apple pulp (can be from Pacific crabapple or haws)
2 cups bitter cherry pulp
5 cups sugar
$1/2$ teaspoon almond extract

Prepare pulp of both fruits first by putting cooked fruit (unsweetened) through a sieve or food mill. Place the pulp in a large saucepan or pot. Heat to a boil, stirring carefully. Add sugar. Stir constantly until it just begins to thicken. Remove from heat. Add extract and blend. Ladle into hot jars. Adjust lids and bands and process in boiling water bath for 5 minutes. Remove from canner.

Yield: 8 half-pints.

Bob Giurgevich, Sheridan, Wyoming

Black Forest Chokecherry Pie

1 9-inch pie shell, baked and cooled. (Refer to page 124 for pie crust recipe, and add to it $1/4$ cup cocoa and 2 tablespoons extra water.)

Chokecherry Pudding Sauce:

2 cups chokecherry juice (from approximately 1 or 2 quarts chokecherries), divided
3 tablespoons cornstarch
1 cup sugar
pinch of salt
$1/2$ teaspoon almond extract

Mix $1/2$ cup juice and cornstarch. Heat $1 1/2$ cups juice with sugar and bring to a boil. Add cornstarch-juice mixture. Cook to thicken. Add salt and extract. Cool.

To make the first layer:

8 ounces cream cheese
$3/4$ cup powdered sugar
$1/3$ of a 12-ounce container of whipped topping

Beat together and spread in shell.

For the second layer:

Pour all but $1/2$ cup of cooled chokecherry pudding sauce into pie over cream cheese mix.

For the third layer:

Beat $1/2$ cup of pudding sauce into half of the 12-ounce whipped topping. Spread over pudding sauce carefully. Use a teaspoon for best results.

You will have a small amount of whipped topping left. Mound the rest of the whipped topping around the edges or all in the center. Sprinkle with slivered chocolate for garnish and place chokecherries on for decoration.

Norma Robertson, Lewistown, Montana
1991 Chokecherry Festival-Best of Show

Chokecherries with Quail or Prairie Chickens

4 quail or 2 prairie chickens or sharp-tailed grouse (cleaned and skinned or plucked)
salt and pepper to taste
2 bay leaves
1 cup water

Place quail, prairie chickens, or grouse in a roaster. Season with salt and pepper, add water and bay leaves, cover, and place in 350-degree oven for 1 hour. Baste every 15 minutes.

Sauce:

1 quart chokecherries, cleaned and washed
4 tablespoons sugar
pinch of cinnamon
1 tablespoon chicken bouillon
currant jelly

(continued on next page)

Clean and drain cherries; grind cherries whole in steel-bladed Osterizer or any grinder. Send through sieve or strainer with small holes. Mix in sugar and simmer for 10 minutes; add a pinch of cinnamon. Add chicken bouillon and simmer a few minutes more.

Pour on quail and put in oven uncovered for 10 minutes. Remove from oven and cover quail with currant jelly until the jelly melts. Serve.

Alma Snell, Fort Smith, Montana

Chokecherry Sauce

1 quart chokecherries
4 tablespoons sugar
1 teaspoon almond extract

Clean and drain cherries; grind cherries whole in steel-bladed Osterizer or any grinder. Send through sieve or strainer with small holes. Mix into the strained cherries, sugar, and almond extract. Simmer for 15 minutes. Remove from heat and use on biscuits like you would jam. Can also use on waffles, pancakes, and ice cream.

Alma Snell, Fort Smith, Montana

Pacific Crab Apple

Crab apples are a group that I have avoided. I guess it's mainly due to the fact that when I think of apples, I usually want one that I can bite into, or peel and core and make into pie or applesauce. It wasn't until Kathy Buchner showed me what a versatile and tasty treat haws (from hawthorns) were that I had to take another look at crab apples.

In the first place, crab apples are bigger than haws so it takes less effort to pick a bucketful of Pacific crab apples than it takes to get a similar amount of haws. Though Pacific crab apple trees sport small spurs, they are not near as threatening as the 2-inch-long thorns that hawthorn presents.

Crab apples have a variety of uses: spiced jelly, apple butter, applesauce. If you collected enough of them, you could probably squeeze them through a press for cider. If you are traipsing about the countryside in autumn and need a little pick-me-up, you can nibble on crab apples; just make sure to spit out the seeds, as they are poisonous.

Pacific crab apples were prized by the Native Americans. They collected the crab apples and stored them in cedar wood storage boxes under water. Because the apples are high in acidity, they store well and only become softer and sweeter with aging. Oftentimes the Native Americans would eat the apples as is, but sometimes they would mash them and mix them with salal.

Though these apples are small, they are tasty and they do make a great sauce or butter. So the next time you are out and about in the fall, pick a peck or so of these tasty little apples and give them a try.

IDENTIFICATION

Pacific crab apple *(Malus fusca)* is a member of the family Rosaceae. It is a shrub or small tree that reaches 6 to 35 feet in height. Pacific crab apples grow in moist, open woods and along the coast from northern California to southern Alaska. They get as far east as the Cascade Mountains in Oregon and Washington.

The branches have numerous thorn-like spurs. The oval-shaped leaves are arranged alternately. The leaves are simple, tapered to a point, with serrated edges. The blossoms occur in April and May, and look just like typical apple blossoms, but smaller. The blossoms are white or pinkish and occur in clusters of 5 to 12 spur shoots. The half-inch-long, oval apples (pome is the botanical term) ripen late August through October. They turn yellow with cheeks of red when ripe. The longer they ripen, the sweeter they are.

Your chances of finding a gallon or two of crab apples is excellent most years. The odds are about nine in ten.

RECIPES

Crab Apple Jelly

5 cups crab apple juice (from approximately 5 pounds crab apples)
7 cups sugar
juice of 1 lemon
5 drops of oil of clove
1 bottle of Certo pectin

Wash the apples thoroughly. Place in large (8-quart) pot. Barely cover with water; boil until the crab apples give off their juice. Drain through a jelly bag.

Combine juice and the sugar. Bring to a full, rolling boil. Add the lemon juice and oil of clove. Add the Certo pectin and boil 1 minute. Pour into jelly jars and seal with lids and screw bands. Process in boiling water bath for 10 minutes.

This makes a delightful jelly that is delicious with meat.

**Modified from Fran Davis' recipe, Otis Orchards, Washington
From *Savoring the Wild*, A Collection of Favorite Recipes from the
Employees of the Montana Department of Fish, Wildlife, and Parks
(Falcon Press, Helena, Montana, 1989)**

Crab Apple Jam

5 quarts crab apples, reduced to 7 cups pulp
2 cups water
$1/4$ cup lemon juice
1 cup apple juice
$1/2$ cup water
1 package pectin
$1\,1/3$ cups honey

Cook crab apples in 2 cups water until they begin to pop (about 20 minutes). Press the cooked crab apples through a sieve or food mill.

(continued on next page)

In a large saucepan or kettle, combine pulp, lemon juice, apple juice, and water. Slowly add pectin. Stir until dissolved. Add honey. Bring to rolling boil. Boil 1 minute. Remove from heat. Pour into sterilized jars, seal, and process 10 minutes in boiling water bath.

Yield: eight 8-ounce jars.

Kathy Buchner, Jackson, Wyoming

Crab Apple Sauce

4 pounds crab apples
2 cups water
2 tablespoons lemon juice
2 cups granulated sugar
1 tablespoon cinnamon
3 drops almond extract

Cook crab apples with water in large covered kettle until they pop. Mash through a sieve. Stir in remaining ingredients.

Modified from a Darcy Williamson recipe,
How to Prepare Common Wild Foods, **Donnelly, Idaho, 1978**

Crab Apple and Plum Butter

3 pounds crab apples
1 pound plums (wild plums are preferred)
1 cup water
1 pound granulated sugar

Wash apples, core, and quarter. Cut plums in half and remove pits. Combine fruit and water; cook until tender. Cool slightly; puree in blender. Add sugar. Cook until thick, stirring constantly. Pour into hot sterilized jars. Process 10 minutes in boiling water bath.

Yield: 3 pints.

Modified from a Darcy Williamson recipe,
How to Prepare Common Wild Foods, **Donnelly, Idaho, 1978**

Crab Apple Mousse

1 cup crab applesauce*
$^1/_2$ cup sugar
1 teaspoon lemon juice and a bit of grated rind (1 teaspoon)
dash of freshly grated nutmeg
dash of salt
1 cup whipping cream

Mix crab apple sauce, sugar, lemon juice and grated rind, nutmeg, and salt. Whip cream and fold into sauce mixture. Pour into ice cube tray and freeze for 2 hours. Place in a well-chilled bowl and beat well. Return to freezer and freeze until firm.

*Haw applesauce can be substituted.

Pat Robinson, Port Hadlock, Washington

Crab Apple Mint Jelly

1 cup mint leaves
1 cup crab apple juice
1 cup sugar

Place mint leaves in a tea strainer or cheesecloth (doubled and tied at the corners). Cover with boiling water and steep for 1 hour. Press juice from leaves and add the mint leaf extract to crab apple juice and sugar; boil until jelly test (see sheet test on page 130) is reached. Put in sterilized jars and seal. Process in boiling water bath for 10 minutes.

You can use multiples of the recipe for bigger batches.

Alma Snell, Fort Smith, Montana

Currant

When currants come to my mind, I think of distinctive tasting jelly and syrup, I see trumpet-shaped flowers, and I smell the spicy perfume of the blossoms. Currants definitely have many pluses, not the least of which is a variety of uses.

The most common currant in the western part of the Northwest is red-flowered currant, while the golden (or black) currant becomes more prominent on the east slope and continues throughout the Rocky Mountain region.

Currants are not my favorite berry to pick, because even the more tasty varieties are not what I would call "hand to mouth" berries. What it means to me is that every currant that I pick goes into the pot—the sooner I pick a gallon, the sooner I can turn it into something tasty. However, currants are quite widespread and usually abundant even when other berries aren't. They also provide a welcome relief for me when I'm guiding fishermen. Since currants are usually growing on the river floodplain, I can slip away for a quarter of an hour and not be missed. The escape I enjoy by doing something mindless eases my irritation and relaxes me. Besides that, I can store the currants that I have picked in my refrigerator for two weeks or so. By that time my 15-minute forays have paid off and I will have gotten between 2 quarts and a gallon.

Rendering currant juice is relatively easy. I just place the currants in an 8-quart pot and add a cup or so of water for each 2 quarts of currants I have. After bringing them to a boil and then simmering them for 15 minutes, I pour the currants into a sieve placed over a bowl or pot. I let the currant juice drain out for about an hour. I might prod the cooked currants with a potato masher a couple of times, but otherwise I leave them alone.

Just like the picked currants, I can store the juice in the refrigerator for weeks so I don't have to make jelly or syrup immediately. In my hectic summer world, that's a mighty important attribute.

᷎᠍

IDENTIFICATION

Currants belong to the family Grossulariaceae and the genus *Ribes*. (Gooseberries belong to the same family and genus.) Currants are shrubs; that is, they have multiple stems. The golden or black currant ranges in height from 3 to 8 feet, while red-flowered currant ranges from 3 to 5 feet.

While many plants can be confusing, there are a few characteristics of currants and gooseberries that make them fairly easy to identify. One is that the berry is globular; that is, it is globe shaped. Second is that there is a "pigtail" attached at the top of the berry (that is, the area opposite the stem). The "pigtail" is the result of the currants having a flower with an inferior ovary (an ovary that is situated below the flower parts). After fertilization the flower parts wither and dry but do not detach from the ovary. The ripe berry still has the flower parts attached, thus giving the "pigtail" appearance.

Another characteristic of members of the Grossulariaceae family is a 3- or 5-lobed leaf that resembles a miniature maple leaf. Red-flowered currant has deep green leaves that are slightly pubescent underneath. Golden or black currant has slightly glossy, light green leaves that are even lighter in color underneath.

Currants blossom in late March through early May, depending on the species and altitude. All have trumpet-shaped flowers arranged in a cluster (raceme) of 6 to 15. The red-flowered currant (*Ribes sanguineum*) is aptly named for its bright red blossoms, while the golden or black currant (*R. aureum*) has a bright yellow flower.

Golden or black currant ripens from mid-July into August. There are two color phases of this currant: gold and black. About four out of five bushes will have black currants. The currants change from light green to light red and, finally, to glossy black as they ripen. Depending on the moisture they receive and the number of currants in the cluster, the size can range from pea- to nearly dime-size. Red-flowered currant ripens from early August into September. The ripe currants are a light, powder blue color and are large pea-size.

R E C I P E S

Currant Jelly

4 cups currant juice (need 2 to 3 quarts of currants)
2 tablespoons lemon juice
3 cups sugar

Clean currants and remove leaves. Don't worry about the stems. Cook slowly in a large saucepan with a small amount of water. Simmer until soft. Crush and strain through a jelly bag. Do not squeeze the bag. Measure 4 cups of juice and pour into a 6- or 8-quart pot. Add lemon juice. Bring to a boil for 3 minutes. Add sugar and stir until completely dissolved. Bring to a boil, stirring constantly. Boil until the jell stage is reached (see sheet test on page 130). Remove from heat, skim off foam and pour into sterilized jars. Place on lids and screw bands securely. Put in a boiling water bath for 10 minutes.

Yield: four 8-ounce jars

Pat Robinson, Port Hadlock, Washington

Currant–Salal Jelly

2 quarts currants to yield $2^1/_2$ cups juice
3 quarts salal to yield $2^1/_2$ cups juice
2 cups water, divided
1 package pectin
$7^1/_2$ cups sugar

Wash and crush the currants in a kettle. In a separate kettle, wash and crush the salal. Add $^3/_4$ cup water to the currants and simmer, covered, for 15 minutes. Add $1^1/_4$ cups of water to the salal and simmer, covered, for 15 minutes. Rest a colander in a bowl or kettle. Spread cheesecloth or a jelly bag to cover the colander. Pour in the hot currants. Fold cloth to form bag and twist from top. Press with potato masher to extract juice. Repeat the process for salal.

Measure $2^1/_2$ cups currant juice and $2^1/_2$ cups salal juice and pour into a 6- or 8-quart kettle. Add pectin and mix thoroughly. Place kettle over high heat. Bring to a boil, stirring constantly. Add sugar and stir. Continue stirring and bring to a full, rolling boil. Boil hard for 2 minutes. Remove from heat, skim off foam, and pour into sterilized jars. Wipe off rims. Use the USDA recommended boiling water bath method. Attach two-piece metal lids securely and place jars in boiling water for 5 minutes.

Dot Heggie, Gillette, Wyoming

Currant and Raspberry Jam

2 cups crushed raspberries (about 3 pints)
2 cups crushed currants (either red-flowering or black)
3 cups sugar

Inspect, wash, thoroughly drain, and crush the raspberries. Wash the currants, remove stems, and crush. Put the raspberries, currants, and sugar into a kettle over low heat and stir until the sugar is dissolved. (If scales are available, use $^3/_4$ pound of sugar to each pound of fruit.) Increase the heat and boil rapidly, stirring constantly, until the juice passes the jelly test (the last drops of juice off the spoon form a sheet or drops fall side by

(continued on next page)

side—see sheet test on page 130). Pour into hot jars and seal. Place in boiling water bath 5 to 10 minutes.

Yield: three 8-ounce jars

Ora Fay Wilson, Martinsdale, Montana

Jelly Roll

1 cup flour
1 teaspoon baking powder
dash of salt
4 eggs
1 teaspoon vanilla
1 jar black currant jelly*

Preheat oven to 375 degrees. Measure and sift dry ingredients into bowl. In another bowl, beat eggs and vanilla together, then add the dry ingredients. Beat by hand until all the flour has been added. Pour onto a greased and floured cookie sheet. Bake for 20 minutes. As soon as the roll is done, remove from the oven and peel back edges of roll from sheet. Invert roll onto a dishtowel that has been sprinkled with powdered sugar.

Cut off crusty edges of roll. Stir up black currant jelly with a knife. Spread the jelly onto roll.

Roll up quickly, using towel as a guide. Remove towel and place jelly roll on a rack (seam side down) to cool.

*This recipe can be used with jelly or jam; chokecherry, blackberry, blueberry, black raspberry, Oregon grape, and elderberry seem to be better choices than others. The black currant's strong, tart taste makes it ideally suited for a jelly roll.

Emily Krumm, Eaton Rapids, Michigan

Elderberry

Elderberry reminds me of autumn, of first frosts and colorful foliage, because these berries ripen in late September through October. My parents, brother, sister, and I would spend a long Sunday afternoon in mid-October scouring the neighboring wood lots for black walnuts and hickory nuts. While we were searching for the nuts, we would often encounter several clumps of elderberry bushes. The tall, pithy canes would be bent over by the masses of elderberries. The BB-sized berries occurred in large clumps (I later found out that the clumps are called cymes).

We would pick the berry clusters and put them in a grocery sack. It was great fun for me to pick these clumps because I felt as though I had gotten so many berries. If it was a good year, we would fill three or four large sacks with the clusters.

I recall those late afternoons as we hiked home: Dad had a gunny sack full of black walnuts, and Mom lugged a smaller bag of hickory nuts, while we kids carried the sacks of elderberries. The late afternoon sun lost its warmth, and my cheeks would turn a rosy red from the cool temperatures. We were happy, though, for we had the makings for a lot of cookies, jelly, and pies—very important items on a child's want list. When we arrived home, we would pull the individual berries off the stems so that Mom could make elderberry jelly or pie—both were great treats.

When I encountered elderberries in the West, I wasn't prepared for the great height that the blue elderberry can reach. Though the canes were somewhat supple, pulling down a 15-foot-high cane to pick the berry clusters often resulted in a broken cane and my feeling like a despoiler.

It wasn't until my friend and next-door neighbor Ora Fay Wilson let me in on her elderberry-picking secret that I could once again pick blue elderberries with no mental problems. Ora Fay told me, "Use a pruner, you know, the one on a long handle with a rope to pull to activate the pruning jaws. I've been able to pick those elderberries that are 10 feet over my head without any problem."

Well, that solved my problem and allowed me to go out and fill two or three grocery bags full of elderberry clusters—just like my childhood days. Now, if I could only convince my mother to visit me during elderberry time so she could make a pie or two.

༂❧

IDENTIFICATION

Elderberry is a shrub that prefers deep, well-drained soils and a moderate amount of sunlight. The stems are more aptly called "canes," for they have a woody exterior and pithy interior. Elderberry can reach heights of 20 feet. The bark is grayish brown with rather prominent lenticels lending an almost wart-like look to the stems.

The leaves are pinnately compound and have from 5 to 7 leaflets that are lance-shaped. The leaflets are toothed, and have a dark green color above, light green below. The flowers are borne in a large, flat-topped inflorescence called a cyme. The creamy white flowers may appear June through July. The berries ripen mid-September through October, turning from green to pale, powdery blue.

Since blue elderberry blossom throughout the summer, there is no chance of losing the flowers to a late spring frost; about the only things that can go wrong are early freezes, birds, and drought. Most of the time (nine out of ten years) you should be able to pick enough for a pie and a batch of jelly.

Caution: Do not eat elderberries raw. Also, avoid picking and using red elderberries. According to Derek Munro, Canadian Poisonous Plants, children have been poisoned when they used the hollow stems of elderberries as whistles. Uncooked berries may cause nausea.

R E C I P E S

Dried Elderberries

Elderberries may be dried and stored for later use in pies, puddings, sauces, etc. The simplest method of drying elderberries is to tie a few cluster stems together with medium-weight string and suspend them over spread newspaper in a moisture-free area for seven to eight days. Remove the dried berries from the stems and store them in tightly covered containers. An alternative method is to remove the elderberries from the stems and spread them on a cookie sheet. Dry in oven set at lowest temperature for 24 hours.

Darcy Williamson, Donnelly, Idaho
How to Prepare Common Wild Foods

Elderberry Sauce

$^1/_2$ cup dried elderberries
$^1/_4$ cup citrus peel, grated
1 cup boiling water
$^3/_4$ cup granulated sugar
1$^1/_2$ teaspoons cornstarch
1 tablespoon margarine
$^1/_2$ teaspoon lemon juice

Simmer elderberries and citrus peel in water over medium heat 45 minutes. Sift sugar and cornstarch together, then add to elderberry mixture. Mix well and continue cooking for 10 minutes. Add margarine and lemon juice.

Good served over gingerbread.

Darcy Williamson, Donnelly, Idaho
How to Prepare Common Wild Foods

Elderberry Rice Pudding

2 cups cooked rice
1$^1/_2$ cups milk
dash of salt
3$^1/_2$ tablespoons granulated sugar
1 tablespoon margarine
1 teaspoon vanilla
2 eggs
$^1/_2$ cup dried elderberries
$^1/_2$ teaspoon lemon rind, grated
1 teaspoon lemon juice

Combine rice, milk, salt, sugar, margarine, vanilla, and eggs. Mix well. Stir in elderberries, rind, and juice. Pour into lightly greased 8 x 8-inch baking pan. Bake at 325 degrees for 1$^1/_2$ hours.

Darcy Williamson, Donnelly, Idaho
How to Prepare Common Wild Foods

Elderberry Wine

Elderberries can be used to make a very good homemade wine. You will need much of the information and ingredients found in the chokecherry wine recipe on page 45. It is best to purchase a wine-making handbook and visit your local brewer's supply store for more information on how best to prepare elderberry wine. Depending on the conditions in which you are working, and the sweetness of your elderberries, any standard wine recipe may need to be adjusted.

Elderberry Wine Jelly

3½ cups elderberry wine
6½ cups sugar
2 teaspoons orange flavor extract
1 bottle liquid pectin

Prepare 8 half-pint canning jars. Mix wine and sugar in large double boiler. Place over boiling water, stirring until sugar is dissolved. Remove from heat and stir in remaining ingredients. Skim off foam as it appears on top. Pour into hot, clean jars. Attach lids and screw rings securely. Process water bath 10 minutes.

Pat Robinson, Port Hadlock, Washington

Gooseberry

While many people don't realize that there are probably gooseberries lurking nearby ready to drag them into a lifelong quest for a puckery berry, I am aware of the temptation and admit that I have succumbed to gooseberry. I confess that I look forward to July and gooseberries.

One of my favorite gooseberry expeditions involved an elderly gentleman, John Orndorff. John was one of my favorite people to guide because he had a lively mind and body, even though he was in his 80s. He had an insatiable curiosity that opened him up to learning every day. John also loved to plan ahead. One of his favorite sayings was, "People my age don't even buy green bananas, but I want to plan a year in advance."

I was guiding John one fine July day. We had stopped on an island. I intended to let John and his partner fish while I picked some gooseberries for dessert (gooseberry dumplings). After placing John and his partner in a couple of hot spots, I told John, "I'm going to pick some gooseberries and I'll be right back."

John promptly replied, "Let me come along and help."

I said, "It's nothing. All I need is 2 cups of gooseberries."

John countered, "I want to see what it's like and then I'll go back to fishing."

Well, John came along and within 40 feet of the boat, I found a gooseberry bush. I showed John what the gooseberry looked like, the distinctive leaves, and the prickly thorns. I also showed John how to pick the half-marble-sized berries by grasping the end of the drooping branch and lifting it up. With the other hand he could pick the dangling berries without so many encounters with the prickles.

In a short while we had 2 cups of gooseberries, so I told John, "We have enough. Let's go."

He bent down, grasped a gooseberry branch and hefted it up. "Oh, look at these! It would be a shame not to pick these beauties."

So we picked the branch and a couple adjacent to it. I announced again, "We have more than enough now. Let's go."

John pulled up another loaded branch and exclaimed, "Look at these! We had better pick them."

John and I picked every loaded branch he found. Instead of coming back with 2 cups of gooseberries, we had 2 quarts! I made gooseberry dumplings at the lunch site and John, a diminutive man of 130 pounds, ate three helpings and then cleaned out the pot! He had gooseberry stains from his chin to his nose and from ear lobe to ear lobe but was he happy.

John passed away in the spring of 1995. I'll forever miss his lively personality and his desire to live each day to the fullest. Every time I float by that island where John and I picked those gooseberries, I remember him and can almost hear him saying, "Oh, look at these beauties."

IDENTIFICATION

Gooseberries and currants have the same identifying characteristics in common: they have trumpet-shaped flowers, globular berries, maple-like leaves, and flower parts retained on the berry. About the only difference between gooseberries and currants is that gooseberries have prickles while currants (or the majority of them, at least) are unarmed.

Gooseberries are shrubs ranging from 3 to 8 feet high and grow in moist areas. In the eastern part of the Northwest, you'll find them in the floodplains of rivers and creeks, and more moist draws and canyons. In the western part of the region, you'll find gooseberries scattered from sea level to mid-range in the mountains. In both areas, gooseberries prefer a moderate amount of shade but can tolerate full sun or full shade, though they don't thrive in either extreme. Gooseberry branches tend to lay over so that the shrub looks rounded. Often the branch will form roots if it touches the ground.

Gooseberries blossom in April to mid-May. The flowers are either light pink or white in color. The blossom has five lobes. Gooseberries ripen in July. The most common western species, *Ribes divarcatum*, turns from light green to light purple, whereas the eastern variety, *R. inerme*, turns from light green to purple. The size of the berry ranges from pea-size to 1 1/2 times pea-size.

While finding enough gooseberries can be challenging on the west slope, many of the east slope spots will yield a gallon to a persistent berry picker in two hours. Your chances of finding a gallon most years are one in four on the west slope and one in two on the east slope.

RECIPES

Gooseberry Dumplings or Slump

Sauce:

> 2 cups gooseberries*
> 1 1/2 cups water
> 3/4 cup sugar

Dumplings:

> 1 cup biscuit mix
> 2 tablespoons sugar
> 1/2 teaspoon nutmeg
> 1/3 cup milk

In a 2- or 3-quart saucepan, mix gooseberries, water, and sugar to make the sauce. Bring to a boil. Cover, reduce heat, and simmer for 10 minutes.

Mix dry ingredients for dumplings. Add milk and mix well with a fork. Drop batter by tablespoonful atop berry mixture. Cook uncovered at low heat for 10 minutes; cover and cook 10 minutes longer. Makes 4 to 6 servings.

*Huckleberries, blueberries, and blackberries can be substituted.

Wilora Dolezal, Cody, Wyoming

"This is a great camp recipe and is my favorite streamside lunch dessert during July." Bob Krumm

Gooseberry–Thimbleberry Jelly

2 quarts thimbleberries*
1/2 cup water, divided
1 quart gooseberries*
4 cups sugar
1/2 package powdered pectin

Stew thimbleberries with 1/4 cup water for 12 minutes. Stew gooseberries with another 1/4 cup water for 12 minutes. Place berries in jelly bag and strain juice. Add sugar to juice and simmer till mixture reaches 220 degrees. Add pectin and boil hard for 1 minute. Pour into sterilized jars, attach lids and screw bands securely. Process in a boiling water bath for 10 minutes.

*Salmonberry, raspberry (red and black), and blackberry can be substituted for thimbleberry; currant or Oregon grape can be substituted for gooseberry.

Darcy Williamson, Donnelly, Idaho
How to Prepare Wild Foods

Gooseberry Pie

$^2/_3$ cup water, divided
2 cups sugar
1$^1/_2$ quarts fresh gooseberries (4 cups if the gooseberries are large)
$^1/_4$ cup cornstarch
pastry for a 2-crust pie (see pie crust recipe on page 124)

Cook $^1/_3$ cup of water and sugar in saucepan over low heat for 2 or 3 minutes. Add berries. Simmer gently about 5 minutes until cooked but still whole. Using a strainer, drain syrup from berries into small pan and place berries in pie shell.

Dissolve cornstarch in remaining $^1/_3$ cup of water. Stir into the syrup. Cook over moderate heat until thick and clear, stirring constantly, about 3 minutes. Cool to lukewarm and pour over berries. Cover with top crust. Bake in 450-degree oven for 10 minutes, then reduce heat to 350 for 35 minutes or until golden brown.

Pauline Deem, Plentywood, Montana

Gooseberry Jelly

Gooseberry Juice:

3 quarts gooseberries
2 quarts water

Wash berries; remove leaves and other trash. Put gooseberries and water in a large kettle. Cook over low heat until berries can be mashed easily. Strain with cheesecloth and gently press through a jelly bag. Hang up bag and allow the juice to slowly drip into kettle. When dripping stops, press the bag gently.

7 cups sugar
5 cups gooseberry juice
1 box powdered pectin

Wash jars; place lids in boiling water; remove from heat. Measure sugar into bowl and set aside. Place gooseberry juice in a 6- to 8-quart pot; stir in pectin. Stirring constantly, bring to a full, rolling boil. Stir in sugar. Stirring constantly, bring to a full, rolling boil and boil for 1 minute. Remove from heat. Skim off foam; pour into sterilized jars, wipe off rims, put on flat lids and screw bands. Invert for 5 minutes. Check seals in 1 hour, or use USDA hot water bath method for 10 minutes.

Judy Heimkes, Brooklyn Park, Minnesota

Gooseberry Trifle

$^1/_3$ cup quick tapioca
2 cups boiling water
2 cups green gooseberries
1 cup sugar
1 tablespoon lemon juice

Cook tapioca in boiling water 15 minutes. Cook gooseberries and sugar until soft. Add lemon juice to gooseberries. Combine mixtures. Chill and serve with ice cream.

Rose Henckel, Milwaukee, Wisconsin

Gooseberry Pudding

3 tablespoons cornstarch
1 cup water
1 quart gooseberries
2 cups sugar

Dissolve cornstarch in water; add gooseberries and sugar. Cook until the mixture is mushy.

Eat as a pudding.

Alma Snell, Fort Smith, Montana

Hawthorn

Many of the berries that I discuss in this book are not only prized by human berry pickers, but by other animals as well. Hawthorn is a good example. Not only is hawthorn prized by raccoons, but also by game birds such as sharp-tailed grouse, ring-necked pheasant, ruffed grouse, and wild turkey. When I'm hunting sharptails and pheasants later in the hunting season, I know that if I find a draw with lots of hawthorn and the bushes are loaded with haws (the little thorn apples or crab apples that grow on hawthorn), I'll find the birds I am after. Another plus of hunting in hawthorn areas is that I can snack on the haws as I chase after my Labrador retriever, Tyrone. The flavor of the haws varies from tree to tree, so if I find a good-tasting haw, I make sure to pick a handful from that tree and then I run to catch up with Ty.

You don't need to worry about keeping the locations of hawthorn secret, because most people don't realize that it makes fine jelly, sauce, and butter. Any recipe you have for crab apples will work on haws.

I seldom go berry picking specifically for hawthorn. I'm usually searching for other berries, but hawthorn seems to pop up when I least expect it, so I take advantage of it. Since hawthorn comes close to being a small tree (15 to 20 feet at times), if you discover a grove near a road, take a small stepladder along to aid in your picking efforts.

You'll not have to venture far from Portland to find haws, because there are plenty of hawthorns along the roadsides, fence lines, and city parks. A couple of the species are used as ornamentals. When these escape, they "creep" outward from where they were planted with the help of birds and mammals dispersing their seeds.

IDENTIFICATION

Though there are at least four species of hawthorns in the Northwest, all will have one characteristic in common: an unbranched thorn. The thorns range from less than $^1/_2$ inch to nearly 3 inches on one species.

Hawthorn is a member of the rose family and the genus *Crataegus*. The two more common species are *Crataegus douglasii* and *C. columbiana*. The former is known as the black hawthorn and the latter goes by the common name of Columbia hawthorn. Two ornamental species, which are commonly found west of the Cascades, are *C. monogyna* and *C. oxyacantha*.

The white to light pink flowers appear in late May through June (depending on altitude) in clusters of about 5 to 20. Each has 5 petals.

The haws, which resemble miniature apples, ripen mid-September through October. At lower elevations, lacking extremely cold winter temperatures, the haws will stay on all winter, unless the birds get them, that is. The black hawthorn has a color of blackish purple when ripe, while the Columbia hawthorn has a color range of yellow, orange, or red.

In the eastern Northwest, you'll find hawthorns growing in more mesic draws and ravines and upper hillsides, especially on the north- and east-facing slopes where there will be more moisture. In the western part of the Northwest, you'll find hawthorns growing along the roadsides, abandoned fields, fence lines, open hillsides, and floodplains of streams.

In most years you should have no problem picking a gallon of haws. This past year, the haw crop was so good you could pick a gallon in 15 minutes, according to my son James.

RECIPES

Hawthorn Jelly

> 1 gallon haws
> water
> sugar

Wash haws and place in a 6- to 8-quart pot. Barely cover with water; simmer until soft. Strain through a jelly bag. Measure juice, place in pot, bring to a rolling boil, skim off foam, and add $3/_4$ cup sugar for each cup of juice. Stir until sugar dissolves, stirring constantly; cook until syrup sheets off spoon (see sheet test on page 130). Seal in hot, sterilized jars. Process in boiling water bath for 10 minutes.

Jeri Mazurek, Woodland, Michigan

Hawthorn Apple Sauce

2 quarts haws*
2 cups water
sugar
cinnamon
nutmeg

Rinse haws and remove stems. Drain and place in a heavy saucepan with water. Cook slowly over low heat until fruit is soft. Run through a Foley food mill to remove skins and seeds. Add sugar, cinnamon, and nutmeg to taste. Put in sterilized pint jars and seal. Boiling water process for 10 minutes.

*Crab apples can also be used.

Pat Robinson, Port Hadlock, Washington

Hawthorn Butter

4 pounds haws (to yield 3 cups of pulp)
1 quart water
7 cups sugar

Cook haws in the water until soft. Press through a sieve. Cook the strained sauce with sugar. Soon after boiling, it will flake rather than coat the spoon. Jar and seal. Process in boiling water bath 10 minutes.

Alma Snell, Ft. Smith, Montana

Hawthorn Butter

4 pounds haws, to yield 3 cups of pulp
water to cover
3 cups sugar
juice of one lemon
$1/4$ teaspoon freshly grated nutmeg

Wash and clean haws, remove stems. Place in a large pot or kettle (6- or 8-quart), cover with water and bring to a boil, then simmer for 15 minutes or until haws are soft and start cracking.

Pour into a sieve that is placed over a large bowl or kettle. Force the pulp through the sieve with a wooden spoon or potato masher.

Measure 3 cups of pulp and place in the large pot or kettle along with sugar and the juice of a lemon. Add nutmeg. Cook until the mixture thickens—about 10 minutes. Pour into hot, sterilized pint jars, attach lids and screw bands, and place in a boiling water bath for 10 minutes.

Darcy Williamson, Donnelly, Idaho
How to Prepare Wild Foods

Highbush Cranberry

Common names can be misleading more often than not. Highbush cranberry is not a true cranberry and doesn't even belong to the family; instead it is a member of the honeysuckle family. Still, if you like the tart taste that cranberry has, you'll no doubt enjoy this berry.

It seems strange to me that this berry is so overlooked by berry pickers, myself included. I have known for the past ten years or so that the berries are edible and that they can be used interchangeably in recipes calling for cranberries, especially when jellies, sauces and catsups are concerned. Maybe my reluctance to go after it wholeheartedly is due to the fact that my mother didn't pick it. If my mother, the queen of all foragers, didn't go after it, it wasn't worth going for.

On further reflection, I can't ever recall seeing many highbush cranberry bushes near our home. Since it grows in moister, almost swampy sites, it didn't have the right environmental conditions to thrive near our home.

Highbush cranberry is one you can pick after the leaves have fallen, for it hangs onto its berries throughout the winter. It is a favorite late season food for many birds that depend on fruit.

The longer highbush cranberries stay on the vine, the sweeter they become. So pick your elderberries, huckleberries, haws, and crab apples first, then go for highbush cranberries; they'll be waiting for you.

❧

IDENTIFICATION

Highbush cranberry (*Viburnum edule & V. opulus*), also known as squashberry, is a shrub that ranges in height from 2 to 12 feet. The bark is smooth with a reddish to gray color. It is a member of the honeysuckle family, Caprifoliaceae.

The shrubs like moist areas and most often are found along river bottoms and the edges of swamps. Both species are widespread in the Northwest.

The leaves are medium green color, hairy underneath, and have 3 lobes with large teeth. The leaves are simple and are arranged oppositely. Highbush cranberry blossoms late May into June depending on the elevation.

The blossom of *V. opulus* is flat-topped (umbel) with larger flowers at the periphery and small, nearly inconspicuous flowers in the center. The entire flower cluster can range from 2 to 6 inches across. The flowers are white. The other species, *V. edule*, has a much smaller blossom of $1/2$ inch to 1 inch across. It is composed of numerous small, white flowers.

During the fall, the leaves of both species turn bright red and the berry turns a bright scarlet color. The berry occurs in clusters of 5 to 20. The berries range in size from pea-size to twice that. The berries persist throughout much of the winter or until the cedar waxwings find them.

RECIPES

Highbush Cranberry Sauce

5$^1/_2$ cups highbush cranberries
4 cups sugar
$^3/_4$ cup water
Slivered, crystallized ginger to taste

Blend all ingredients in a saucepan and bring to a full, rolling boil. Boil until a little of the juice will jell on the spoon (about half an hour). Pour into sterilized jelly glasses and seal with lids and screw bands. Place in a boiling water bath for 10 minutes.

Pat Robinson, Port Hadlock, Washington

Highbush Cranberry Mayonnaise

$^1/_4$ cup highbush cranberry sauce
1 teaspoon lemon juice
$^1/_2$ cup mayonnaise

Crush berries in the sauce with a fork and gently blend sauce, lemon juice, and mayonnaise.

Pat Robinson, Port Hadlock, Washington

Highbush Cranberry Catsup

3 pounds highbush cranberries
$^3/_4$ pound sweet onions
1$^1/_2$ cups water
1$^1/_2$ cups cider vinegar
3 cups sugar
2 teaspoons cinnamon
1 teaspoon cloves
1 teaspoon salt
2 stalks finely chopped celery
2 teaspoons pepper

(continued on next page)

Cook berries and onions in water until soft. Put through a sieve and return pulp to the saucepan. Add remaining ingredients. Bring to a boil and reduce heat, cooking until sauce is typical catsup consistency. Stir constantly and be careful not to scorch. Use a heat defuser and take your time. Pour into sterilized jars and seal immediately. Process in a boiling water bath 10 minutes.

Pat Robinson, Port Hadlock, Washington

Cranberry Catsup Meat Loaf

I pound ground antelope, deer, or elk
I pound lean ground pork
2 eggs
1 $^1/_2$ cups cracker crumbs
I large chopped onion
$^1/_2$ chopped green bell pepper
I tablespoon horseradish
$^1/_2$ teaspoon salt
I tablespoon mustard
$^1/_2$ cup highbush cranberry catsup (see previous recipe)
I cup cranberry sauce

Throw all ingredients together, except the cranberry sauce, into a large mixing bowl and mix well—make sure you have clean hands! Shape into a bread pan and bake I hour at 350 degrees. Spread cranberry sauce over the meat loaf and return to oven for another 10 minutes.

Pat Robinson, Port Hadlock, Washington

Highbush Cranberry Jelly

2 quarts highbush cranberries
$^1/_2$ cup water
1 package powdered pectin
6 cups sugar

Crush ripe berries. Add water. Simmer 10 minutes. Strain out juice. To 4 cups juice add powdered pectin. Stir in thoroughly. Heat to boiling and stir for 1 minute. Add sugar. Boil hard for 1 minute, stirring constantly. Skim and pour into hot, sterilized jars. Seal. Process in hot water bath 10 minutes.

Charlotte Heron, Choteau, Montana

Highbush Cranberry Syrup

2 cups highbush cranberry juice (from approximately 1 quart highbush cranberries)
2 cups sugar
2 cups white corn syrup

Extract juice as for jelly. Heat juice to boiling, add sugar, stir until dissolved. Add corn syrup, heat to boiling, and simmer about 5 minutes. Seal in hot, sterilized jars. Delicious on ice cream, pancakes, or waffles.

Sharon Henry, Fort Smith, Montana

Oregon Grape

Common names fascinate me. How did a member of the barberry family end up being called a grape? The leaves are quite leathery with bristles at the edges. To me, it looks more like holly than any grape I know. Still, if you look at a cluster of the berries with their pale blue color, it is quite easy to see why they were called grapes.

Oregon grape is one that I do not recommend a person eat as is. It's not that the fruit is poisonous, it's just that it has quite a vile taste. Amazingly, it makes a good jelly. I guess it just proves what a forager friend, Sam Ristich, once told me: "You can make jelly out of practically any plant—if you add enough sugar!"

James contends that Oregon grape is a great thirst quencher on a hot day. Just pop a couple into your mouth and chew. Spit out the seeds and skins after you've swallowed the juice.

Oregon grape is quite widespread throughout the Northwest and it is relatively easy to pick large quantities of it. I was amazed at the heavy crops of grapes that occurred on the plants I saw in the Coastal and Cascade ranges. Many of the plants held over 30 grapes—a far cry from what I have been used to.

Blackberry blossoms

JAMES KRUMM

Cut-leaf Blackberry blossom
(note leaves for this species)

Blackberries

Blackcap Raspberry blossom

STOWELL & SKEAN

Blackcap Raspberries

Blueberry blossoms

Oval-leaf Blueberries

Red Huckleberries

Chokecherry blossom

Bitter Cherries

Pacific Crabapple blossoms

Pacific Crabapples

AARON LIESTON

Red Currant blossoms
(Black Currant blossoms are
similar, except they are
yellow.)

Black Currants

Red Currants

Elderberry blossoms

JAMES KRUMM

Red Elderberries

Blue Elderberries

Gooseberry blossom

Gooseberries

Hawthorn blossoms

Hawthorn berries

STOWELL & SKEAN

Highbush Cranberry blossoms

Highbush Cranberries

JAMES KRUMM

Oregon Grape blossoms

Oregon Grapes

Red Raspberry blossom

Red Raspberries

Wild Rose blossom

Wild Rose Hips

Salal blossoms

Salal berries

AARON LIESTON

Salmonberry blossom

JAMES KRUMM

Red Salmonberry

JAMES KRUMM

Yellow Salmonberry

Serviceberry blossoms

Serviceberries

Wild Strawberry blossoms

Wild Strawberry

Thimbleberry blossom

James Krumm

Thimbleberries

Woody Nightshade
(poisonous, see page 11)

Baneberry
(poisonous, see page 11)

JAMES KRUMM

Japanese Yew
(poisonous, see page 12)

TODD DAVIS PHOTOGRAPHY

Holly
(poisonous, see page 12)

Poison Ivy
(poisonous, see page 13)

JAMES KRUMM

Poison Oak
(poisonous, see page 13)

My experience with Oregon grape has been limited to patches in the Bighorn Mountains. It seemed that I could find quite a few plants but very few grapes in what I had been told was the right vegetation zone, namely, ponderosa pine. One day in early August, I was walking my dogs near Fort Smith, Montana, and stumbled upon a substantial patch of Oregon grape at a lower altitude and earlier in the year than what I had expected. For the first time, I was able to pick enough for a couple batches of jelly.

Unfortunately, the place was not only loaded with Oregon grape but there were rattlesnakes about and quite a concentration of poison ivy. Since I am scared to death of the former and allergic to the latter, I had to be very careful where and how I picked. After I got back, I washed my hands and arms with lots of soap to rid myself of any poison ivy I might have picked up. Luckily, all I got from the berry expedition was a batch of Oregon grape jelly.

Oregon grape is so common in the Northwest that a good berry picker should be able to get a gallon or more each berrying trek.

❧

I D E N T I F I C A T I O N

There are three species of Oregon grape in the Northwest: *Mahonia repens*, *M. nervosa*, and *M. aquifolium*. The list runs from the shortest to the tallest species. *M. Repens* rarely exceeds 6 inches in height, *M. nervosa* about 18 inches, and *M. aquifolium* 3 to 4 feet. Incidentally, *M. nervosa* is Oregon's state flower.

All three resemble one another with leathery, pinnately compound leaves with spiny margins. The leaflets resemble holly leaves. The number of leaflets varies according to the species: 5 to 7 for the low-lying *repens* and up to 15 for the other two.

Oregon grape blossoms early in the spring. The bright yellow blossoms are arranged in clusters called racemes. The powder-blue berries ripen from August to mid-September, even later for those plants growing at higher altitudes. The berries are about the size of peas to small marbles.

You'll find Oregon grape growing from sea level up to dry mountain slopes. Oregon grape thrives in moderate sunlight and does quite well in thinned timber stands and recently logged areas. In the eastern areas of the Northwest, it is commonly found in open stands of ponderosa pine.

RECIPES

Oregon Grape Jelly

> 4 cups Oregon grape juice (from approximately 3 quarts Oregon grapes)
> 1 tablespoon lemon juice
> 3 cups sugar

Clean grapes and cook in large (6- to 8-quart) saucepan or pot with a small amount of water. Simmer until hot and juicy. Crush and strain through a jelly bag. Do not squeeze bag. Return juice to clean pan, add lemon juice, and boil for 3 minutes. Add sugar and stir until dissolved. Bring to a boil while constantly stirring. Check for jell stage after 4 minutes (see sheet test on page 130). Pour into sterilized jars and attach lids and rings securely. Process in boiling water bath for 10 minutes.

Yield: five to six 1-cup jars of jelly.

Pat Robinson, Port Hadlock, Washington

Oregon Grape Wine

Oregon grapes can be used to make a very good homemade wine. You will need much of the information and ingredients found in the chokecherry wine recipe on page 45. It is best to purchase a wine-making handbook and visit your local brewer's supply store for more information on how best to prepare Oregon grape wine. Depending on the conditions in which you are working and the sweetness of your Oregon grapes, any wine recipe will need to be adjusted.

Oregon Grape Wine Jelly

$3^1/_2$ cups Oregon grape wine
$6^1/_2$ cups sugar
2 teaspoons orange flavor extract
1 bottle liquid pectin

Prepare 8 half-pint jelly jars. Mix wine, sugar, and orange flavor extract in large double boiler. Place over boiling water, stirring until sugar is dissolved. Remove from heat and stir in pectin. Skim if foam appears. Pour into hot, clean jars and attach lids and rings securely. Place in a boiling water bath for 10 minutes.

Yield: eight 8-ounce jars.

Pat Robinson, Port Hadlock, Washington

Oregon Grape–Apple Jelly

2 cups Oregon grape juice (from approximately 2 quarts of Oregon grapes)
2 cups apple juice concentrate
1 package MCP pectin
$4^1/_2$ cups sugar

Add juices to a kettle; stir in pectin until it dissolves. Place over high heat; bring to boil, stirring constantly to avoid scorching. Add sugar; mix well. Continue stirring and bring to a full, rolling boil (a boil that cannot be stirred down). Boil hard exactly 2 minutes. Remove from heat. Skim foam and pour into hot, sterilized jars to within $^1/_8$ inch of top. Place lids on jars, tighten bands, place in a hot water bath, and boil for 10 minutes.

Charlotte Heron, Choteau, Montana

Raspberry

Raspberry is my hiking favorite. Whether it is a day hike to my favorite trout stream or a weeklong affair, it seems that my energy levels are restored by that tasty little berry.

One of my favorite hikes leads me down into a canyon with several talus slopes, a small creek and its associated floodplain, and an old logging operation complete with sluice and rusty old steam engine. The hike is ostensibly so that I can fish the river at the bottom of the canyon, but I know, too, that there are plenty of tasty stops along the 1³/₄-mile jaunt. Each talus slope has several raspberry patches that need to be inspected.

The mountain creek has created open, gravelly areas that are quickly inhabited by raspberry bushes. These sites need to be inspected lest I let one of those tasty morsels escape. The old logging operation also created a lot of open space. Rock dams were used to back up water for the sluice. Those dams still hold a patch or two of raspberries. Why, there are even a few raspberry bushes growing around the old steam engine.

If you have never eaten wild raspberries, then you don't know that these cousins of the tame variety are about four times more flavorful and actually not much smaller than the cultivar.

Anyway, the supreme taste of these wild berries makes it more than worth my while to take little detours as I hike to the river.

When I finally arrive at the river, I assemble my fly rod and put on a grasshopper pattern. A rainbow trout attacks the fly on my first cast. While the rainbow isn't a monster, it is pretty, well-colored, and full of fight. I release it and continue on. I know that this is going to be a great day of fishing, for the trout are eager and there are several raspberry patches between me and my upstream destination. It doesn't get any better than good fishing and good berry picking.

IDENTIFICATION

The most common species of raspberry is *Rubus idaeus*. Raspberry is a shrub that prefers disturbed areas such as timber cuts, talus slopes, burns, and stream floodplains, in the mid- to high ranges of the mountains. In the Northwest, raspberry is more common on the east side of the Cascades into Montana and Idaho.

Raspberries are biennials, that is, each cane (stem) lives two years. The rootstock sends up shoots each year which turn into canes. The second year canes branch out a bit, blossom, and bear fruit. Shortly after the berries ripen, the canes die.

The canes have small thorns or prickles. Some clumps of raspberry bushes will have few prickles, while other clumps will have so many prickles that the stems look "hairy." The height of raspberry ranges from 18 inches to 3 feet.

Wild raspberry leaves are pinnately compound (that is, the leaflets are arranged along the main axis of the leaf) with either 3 or 5 leaflets. The oval leaflets are pointed at the tip with whitish undersides.

Raspberry blossoms from June into July—the higher the altitude, the later it blossoms. The white-petaled flowers occur in loose clusters of 4 to 10.

Raspberry ripens late July through mid-September—again, depending on the altitude. The half-sphere-shaped berries are red and about half the size of a domestic raspberry. If you have ever seen domestic raspberries, you'll have no trouble identifying the wild variety—it's just a smaller version of its domesticated cousin.

While raspberries are tasty, they are not plentiful. The small shrubs don't produce that many berries in most years. Consequently, your chances of getting 2 quarts of raspberries—enough for a batch of jam—are slim. You probably only have a 10 percent chance of ever picking 2 quarts. Your chances of getting 2 cups is probably two out of three. However, you can make a lot of tasty things with 2 cups, so go for it.

RECIPES

Wild Raspberry Dressing

$^1/_3$ cup wild raspberries, crushed and lightly sugared*
$^1/_4$ cup mayonnaise
$^1/_2$ cup sour cream

Mix all ingredients together and serve on fruit salad. Keep dressing refrigerated.

*Strawberries, blackcaps, thimbleberries, and salmonberries may be substituted.

Pat Robinson, Port Hadlock, Washington

Grandma's Dessert

4 eggs
1 cup milk
1 teaspoon vanilla
4 tablespoons flour
4 to 6 tablespoons sugar
1 to 1$^1/_2$ cups raspberries

Beat eggs. Blend milk, vanilla, flour, and sugar together. Beat eggs into the milk mixture. Fold in raspberries. Pour into custard baker or individual custard cups. Place the molds in a pan of water in the oven at 325 degrees for 45 minutes or until custard is set.

Pat Robinson, Port Hadlock, Washington

Raspberry Pancakes

> 2 cups dry pancake mix
> 1$^3/_4$ cup water
> $^1/_2$ cup red raspberries

Blend together pancake mix and water. Add raspberries. Pour batter onto greased griddle or frying pan over medium heat. Turn when bubbles in batter start to break and the edges start to dry.

Makes 12-14 pancakes.

Bob Krumm, Sheridan, Wyoming

I prefer using Krusteaz Pancake Mix for this recipe. The recipe is a great one for a backpacker's breakfast, especially when coupled with the syrup recipe below.

Raspberry Syrup

> 1 cup water
> $^1/_2$ cup brown sugar
> $^1/_2$ cup red raspberries

Combine the ingredients. Bring to a boil, then simmer for 5 minutes or longer. Serve over hot pancakes.

Bob Krumm, Sheridan, Wyoming

Very Berry Sorbet

I envelope unflavored gelatin
$^1/_2$ cup sugar
I $^1/_2$ cups water
2 cups pureed raspberries*
$^1/_2$ cup creme de cassis or cranberry juice
2 tablespoons lemon juice

In a medium-sized saucepan, mix gelatin with sugar. Blend in water. Let stand I minute. Stir over low heat till completely dissolved. Let cool to room temperature. Stir in remaining ingredients. Pour into a 9-inch baking pan and freeze for 3 hours or till firm. With electric mixer or food processor, beat till smooth. Return to pan and freeze 2 more hours or till firm. To serve, let thaw at room temperature 15 minutes or until slightly soft. Makes 8 servings.

*Strawberries, blackberries, black raspberries, salmonberries, thimbleberries, juneberries, or huckleberries can be substituted.

The *Missoulian*, 1985
Submitted by Charlotte Heron, Choteau, Montana

Raspberry Ricotta Pie

pastry for I-crust pie (see pie crust recipe on page 124)
2$^1/_2$ cups fresh raspberries
$^3/_4$ cup sugar, divided
I $^1/_2$ tablespoons quick-cooking tapioca
$^1/_2$ teaspoon cinnamon
8 ounces ricotta cheese
I egg, separated
$^1/_4$ teaspoon salt
$^1/_2$ cup half-and-half
I tablespoon lemon juice
$^3/_4$ teaspoon grated lemon peel

Preheat oven to 425 degrees. Line 9-inch pie plate with pastry. In bowl, combine berries, sugar, tapioca, and cinnamon until blended. Let stand 5 minutes.

Place in a blender: ricotta, egg yolk, salt, half-and-half, remaining sugar, and lemon juice plus peel. Blend until pureed.

In a separate bowl, beat egg white until soft peaks form. Fold into cheese mixture, just enough to blend.

Spoon berry mixture into baked shell, then spread cheese mixture over fruit. Sprinkle with cinnamon. Bake for 10 minutes, until topping appears firm when you shake dish gently.

Janet Belanger, Buckfield, Maine

Raspberry Sauce

1 pint pureed raspberries*
$^1/_2$ cup red currant jelly
1 tablespoon lemon juice
5 teaspoons cornstarch, blended with 3 tablespoons cold water

Combine. Cook and stir until clear, about 3 minutes. Cool and serve over ice cream or cake.

*Blueberries, huckleberries, salmonberries, thimbleberries, black raspberries, and blackberries may be substituted.

From *Huckleberry Time*

Rose

Wild rose has been a favorite of mine for a long time, probably because I can enjoy it twice: once in the spring when it blossoms and fills the air with its heavenly fragrance, and again in early fall when the hips ripen so that I can pick them to use in tea, jelly, and other tasty recipes.

Rose is a common plant that is found nationwide. I doubt that any mainland state does not have at least one species of wild rose growing within its borders. Most states will have four or more species.

In today's world of health-conscious people and trends for eating right, wild rose is a natural. Twenty or more years ago a vitamin manufacturer started making vitamin C capsules from rose hips. I had known for a long time that rose hips were high in vitamin C, but I didn't realize that rose hips contained the most vitamin C of any natural source.

I also read that mountain men used to eat rose hips as emergency rations, but I knew very little else about them until I started picking them, more or less just to nibble on as I was hiking about on a bird-hunting trip or waiting on an angler. I found that the taste can range from bland to tasty from bush to bush. Once I found a bush that had a good-tasting hip, I knew the rest would be, too. I like to nibble the skin off and toss the core of hairy seeds—it's a fine line between tasty skin and those hairy seeds—but most of the time I can manage.

You don't have to pick rose hips when they ripen in August along with a lot of other berries; they'll still be there come October, so save your rose hip foray for then.

IDENTIFICATION

One sure identifying feature of this shrub is that it has thorns or prickles. Depending on the species, rose can range from 6 inches to 8 feet high. Rose has pinnately compound leaves with 5 to 11 leaflets. The leaflets have large teeth.

Rose blossoms in June. The petals can range in color from nearly white to deep pink, and from $1/2$ inch to 1 inch long. The seeds are enclosed in a fleshy cup, or hip, that turns orange or red when it ripens in September and October.

There are very few years that you can't get a bucketful of rose hips. Your chances of getting 2 gallons are about nine out of ten.

RECIPES

Candied Rose Hips

1 pound rose hips
2 cups sugar

Spread cleaned and seeded rose hips in a greased 9 x 13-inch pan. Sprinkle with sugar and let stand 1 hour. Stir. Cover with foil and bake at 350 degrees for 45 to 50 minutes. Stir occasionally while cooking by lifting foil and turning rose hips with a metal spatula. Chill until ready to use.

Pat Robinson, Port Hadlock, Washington

Rose Hip Upside Down Cake

1 tablespoon butter
$1/4$ cup brown sugar
$1/2$ cup candied rose hips (see previous recipe)
white or yellow cake mix

In an 8 x 8-inch pan, melt butter and brown sugar. Remove from heat and add candied rose hips evenly over mixture. Prepare batter of a small white or yellow cake mix according to the directions and pour over rose hip mixture. Bake in moderate (350-degree) oven for 30 minutes or as recommended in the cake mix directions. Remove from oven, cool 2 minutes, then invert onto serving plate.

Pat Robinson, Port Hadlock, Washington

Rose Hip Puree

2 pounds cleaned rose hips, seeds remaining
2 pints water

Cook rose hips in water until tender. Press mixture through sieve. Heat puree, pour into jars, attach lids and rings securely, and place in boiling water bath for 10 minutes.

Pat Robinson, Port Hadlock, Washington

Rose Hip Honey

2 pints of rose hip puree (see previous recipe)
1 pound of sugar
1 tablespoon lemon juice

Boil until soft and thickened. Pour into sterilized jars, attach lids and rings securely, and place in a boiling water bath for 10 minutes. Store in a cool, dry place.

Pat Robinson, Port Hadlock, Washington

Rose Hip Jelly

  I pound rose hips
  2 cups water
  lemon juice
  sugar

Put rose hips in a heavy pan (6- to 8-quart) with water. Boil until the hips are soft. Strain through a Foley food mill and then a jelly bag. Do not squeeze the jelly bag. Measure the juice and return it to the pan. Add 3 tablespoons of lemon juice for every 2 cups of rose hip juice. For every 2 cups of rose hip juice use 1 1/2 cups sugar (3 parts sugar for every 4 parts juice). Boil for 10 minutes while stirring constantly. Test to see if the jelling point has been reached (see sheet test on page 130). Pour into sterilized jars. Attach lids and bands securely and place in a boiling water bath for 10 minutes.

Pat Robinson, Port Hadlock, Washington

Rose Hip Soup (Scandinavian Soup)

  2 cups fresh rose hips (seeds remaining)
  I quart water
  $1/2$ cup sugar
  cornstarch paste (I tablespoon plus a little water)

Boil until rose hips are tender. Put through sieve. Add enough water to make I quart again. Stir in sugar and cornstarch paste. Cook until sugar is dissolved and cornstarch has thickened mixture and cleared. Serve hot or cold with a glop of sour cream floating on top!

Pat Robinson, Port Hadlock, Washington

Salal

This member of the heath family has such illustrious relatives as blueberry, huckleberry, cranberry, and wintergreen. In all my readings and conversations about edible berries, it seems that salal was never mentioned. It wasn't until my son, James, mentioned that salal was abundant in Oregon and that we should include it when we got around to writing another berry book. After I discovered salal, I thought it was a shame that it didn't enjoy greater popularity. It is quite abundant and has an excellent flavor, much like the delicate, mild-tasting serviceberry.

When Dot and I traveled about Oregon and Washington, we encountered salal everywhere, or so it seems. One place it was extremely abundant was in the recent timber cuts in the Coastal Range. Pat and Larry Robinson took us to a place that had been logged two or three years previously. Much of the slash still remained and the young coniferous trees were already 3 to 4 feet tall. Salal seemed to make up 60 percent of the ground cover.

It was such an easy matter to pick handfuls of salal berries because of the clusters in which they occur. (I later read that it is okay to pick the cluster and use the entire cluster to make juice.) Many times some of the berries would "slip" and I would end up with just the skin, but there was enough juice and substance to whet my appetite.

One place that really was loaded with salal was on the north end of Highway 101 where the highway meets the ocean. Dot and I had stopped to admire the scenery, which was beyond belief. Just beyond the shore, there were islands getting pounded by the surf. The shoreline was a crazy bunch of jackstraws, only the straws were 30- to 40-foot logs that had been tossed ashore by the waves.

We tried to drink it all in, but it was too much. As we walked back to the car, I realized that the hiking trail was lined with salal. Every branch had two or three heavy, black clusters. Though we were in a hurry, we couldn't pass up the succulent berries that were within arm's reach. We picked enough to fill up my baseball cap and decided to go. The berries, coupled with ones we had picked earlier in the day, filled our gallon bucket to overflowing.

I don't think I have ever picked berries in more awesome surroundings or witnessed bushes as heavily loaded. Dot and I departed with deep regret for we both could have easily spent a week roaming about the ocean shore and enjoying its berries and scenic wonders.

IDENTIFICATION

Salal, *Gaultheria shallon*, is a member of the family Ericaceae, which includes blueberries, huckleberries, and cranberries, to name a few.

Salal is a shrub that can reach 10 feet in height but can trail out along the ground, too. It can form dense thickets in the coniferous woods. In order to thrive, it needs a moderate amount of sunlight.

The simple leaves are rather thick and leathery with serrated edges. The oval leaves have a bit of "drip tip," i.e., they suddenly taper to a narrow tip, and are dark green on top and light green underneath. The leaves are approximately 2 inches long. The flowers are urn-shaped and pale pink in color. The berries are black with rather thick, rough skin. Reddish stems support the berries. The part of the berry opposite the stem (whether you call it the top or bottom) has a cross-like indentation. The berries are about a quarter-inch across.

You can find salal from British Columbia south to southern California and east to the east slope of the Cascades. It occurs in the lowlands up into the lower mountains. Salal grows from sea level to 2,500 feet. It blossoms May to June (I've even found blossoms in August) and ripens from August through mid-October.

Your chances of finding a gallon or two of salal are about 100 percent. Salal is a very common berry in the western Northwest.

R E C I P E S

Boiled Salal Cake

Cake:

- 1 pound salal berries
- 2 cups water
- $^{1}/_{2}$ cup butter
- 1 cup cold water
- $^{1}/_{2}$ cup sugar
- 4 cups flour
- 2 teaspoons baking soda
- $^{1}/_{4}$ teaspoon nutmeg
- $^{1}/_{4}$ teaspoon cinnamon
- 1 teaspoon vanilla

Simmer berries in 2 cups water for 10 minutes. Let mixture cool. Mix together butter and cold water. Add sugar. Beat in flour, baking soda, nutmeg, cinnamon, and vanilla. Add cooled salal to mixture. Bake at 350 degrees for 45 minutes or until done.

Sour cream icing:

- 1 cup sour cream
- $^{3}/_{4}$ cup sugar
- $^{3}/_{4}$ cup brown sugar

Combine and boil until soft stage. Let cool. Beat until creamy. Add 1 teaspoon vanilla. Frost cooled cake.

Pat Robinson, Port Hadlock, Washington

Salal–Bitter Cherry Jelly

2 cups salal juice (from approximately 2 quarts berries)
2 cups bitter cherry or chokecherry juice
    (from approximately 2 quarts cherries)
1/4 cup lemon juice
1 package powdered pectin
5 cups sugar

Extract juice of the salal and cherries by washing them and then placing them in separate pots with 1 cup water for each quart of berries. Bring to a boil and then simmer for 15 minutes. Place in a jelly bag and squeeze gently. Measure juice.

Place cherry and salal juices in a 6- or 8-quart pot along with lemon juice and pectin. Stir until pectin is dissolved. Place over high heat and bring to a full, rolling boil. Add sugar and bring back to a full, rolling boil while stirring constantly. Boil for 1 minute, skim off foam, and pour into hot, sterilized jars. Place on lids and secure bands. Put in a boiling water bath for 10 minutes.

Yield: eight 8-ounce jars

Pat Robinson, Port Hadlock, Washington

Salal–Oregon Grape Jelly

2 cups salal juice (from approximately 2 quarts berries)
2 cups Oregon grape juice (from approximately 2 quarts grapes)
1/4 cup lemon juice
1 package powdered pectin
5 cups sugar

Extract the juice from the salal berries and Oregon grapes. Pour the measured juices into a large 6- or 8-quart pot. Add lemon juice and pectin. Stir until pectin is dissolved. Place over high heat and bring to a full, rolling boil. Add pre-measured sugar. Bring back to a full, rolling boil while stirring constantly. Continue boiling and stirring for 1 minute. Remove from heat, skim off foam, and pour into hot, sterilized jelly jars. Place on lids and attach screw bands. Put in a boiling water bath for 10 minutes.

Yield: eight 8-ounce jars

Pat Robinson, Port Hadlock, Washington

Salal Jelly

3 quarts salal berries
2 cups water
$^1/_2$ cup lemon juice, divided
1 package powdered pectin
6 cups sugar

Clean and wash salal berries. Place in a 6- or 8-quart pot, add water and $^1/_4$ cup lemon juice. Bring to a boil. Simmer 10 minutes. Extract juice by placing three layers of cheesecloth (or jelly bag) over a sieve or colander. Wrap up ends of cheesecloth. Press with spoon or potato masher.

Measure $4^1/_2$ cups salal juice into pot, add pectin and remaining $^1/_4$ cup lemon juice. Stir until dissolved. Bring to a rolling boil, stirring constantly. Add sugar. Bring to a full, rolling boil while stirring constantly. Boil 2 minutes. Remove from heat, skim, pour into sterilized jars and attach lids and screw bands. Process in boiling water bath 10 minutes.

Yield: seven 8-ounce jars.

Dot Heggie, Gillette, Wyoming

Salmonberry

Salmonberry strikes me as a raspberry that turned yellow and decided to grow up a bit. After picking a lot of red raspberries as a child and then encountering salmonberries at this stage of my life, I can only say that I wish someone had crossed salmonberries and raspberries, because salmonberries are so much bigger and easier to pick.

Salmonberry seems to like moister areas. The ones I found were along streams and the edges of marshes. That suits me just fine; any berries that grow close to water make it easier for me to snack while I fish.

Dave Hughes and his wife, Masako Tani, love to fish and to forage. I think that they will probably try to combine trips to their favorite streams and lakes to coincide with the ripening of salmonberries. Since the berries are so close to water, they won't have to be far away, just in case the big trout start feeding.

While there are those berry pickers who will contend that salmonberries aren't worth the trouble, that they are watery and insipid and not nearly as good-tasting as huckleberries or blueberries, I would counter that every person has favorites, and salmonberry has become one of mine.

IDENTIFICATION

Salmonberries resemble raspberries in a lot of ways, and rightly they should for they are in the same family, Rosaceae, and genus, *Rubus*. Salmonberry has the scientific name of *Rubus spectabilis*. Salmonberry prefers more moist areas than raspberry; I found some growing in a very moist area along the borrow pit of a road just south of Mount Hood.

Salmonberry grows as high as 12 feet, again taller than raspberry on the average. Most salmonberry plants fall in the 5 to 8 foot range. The bark is a dark, golden brown and somewhat shredded. Prickles are not numerous.

The leaves are arranged alternately and are compound with three leaflets. The leaflets are markedly toothed and shaped somewhat like a spade.

The brilliantly bright, red or pink flowers occur in late April through May. The flowers can be as much as an inch and a quarter across. There are usually one or two per stem.

The berries ripen mid-July to mid-August. There are two colors: yellow and red. Both are rather soft and slightly larger than the typical blackcap or red raspberry. The flavor is mild but very tasty with a hint of citrus flavor.

Your chances of finding a quart of salmonberries are 50/50 due to the fact that there are so few berries per plant. Since salmonberries often grow in large thickets, your chances are enhanced if you hit it at the peak of the season. A lot of scouting will pay off if you are serious about getting a lot of salmonberries.

RECIPES

Salmonberry Jam

6 cups crushed salmonberries
1 tablespoon lemon juice
1 package pectin
9 cups sugar

(continued on next page)

Clean and crush berries. Place in heavy 8-quart pot. Add lemon juice and pectin. Stir in well. Place over high heat and bring to a boil while stirring constantly. Add sugar and continue to stir constantly. Bring to a full, rolling boil. Boil hard for 4 minutes. Remove from heat and skim any foam. Ladle immediately into clean jars. Seal with lids and rings and invert jars for 10 minutes. (Or place in a hot water bath and bring to a boil for 10 minutes).

Pat Robinson, Port Hadlock, Washington

Salmonberry Jelly

3 quarts firm salmonberries
1 package pectin
4$^1/_2$ cups sugar

Wash berries, place in a large pan, crush, heat to a boil, then simmer 5 minutes; place in jelly bag and squeeze out juice. Add a little water or orange juice if needed to make 3$^1/_2$ cups juice. Put in heavy pan and add pectin. Stir constantly over high heat until mixture comes to a boil. Stir in sugar and return to a full, rolling boil. Boil 2 minutes and skim off foam, then pour into clean, sterilized jars. Put on lids and rings and place in a boiling water bath for 10 minutes.

Pat Robinson, Port Hadlock, Washington

Salmonberry Jam

salmonberries*
sugar

Wash and pick over salmonberries. Measure. Combine with two-thirds of that amount of sugar. Stir mixture over moderate heat until sugar dissolves. Turn to high heat; bring mixture to a boil until it has a thick consistency and the berries become clear. Stir constantly. When the jam sheets off a spoon, the jell stage has been reached. Pour into hot, sterilized jars; put on lids and bands. Place in boiling water bath for 10 minutes.

*Blackcaps, blackberries, and raspberries may be substituted.

Dot Heggie, Gillette, Wyoming

Salmonberry Cake

2 cups flour
$^1/_2$ teaspoon salt
3 teaspoons baking powder
$^1/_3$ cup butter or margarine
1 cup sugar
1 egg
1 cup milk
1 teaspoon vanilla
2 cups salmonberries*

Mix flour, salt, and baking powder. Cream butter and sugar; add egg. Add dry ingredients alternately with milk and vanilla to butter mixture. Pour into greased 9 x 13-inch pan; sprinkle with salmonberries. Bake at 375 degrees for about 30 minutes.

Frosting:

1 $^1/_2$ cups powdered sugar
1 teaspoon melted butter
3 tablespoons cream or milk

Combine all frosting ingredients and mix. Frost cake while it is still warm.

*Raspberries, black raspberries, thimbleberries, or blackberries can be substituted.

Betty Close, Kiel, Wisconsin

Serviceberry

While many berry pickers actively seek huckleberries and blueberries, few, if any, go after the delectable serviceberry (aka juneberry or shad bush). Though serviceberry is quite common, it just doesn't attract the crowd of berry pickers that the other berries do. It's a shame these folks don't realize that serviceberry has a uniquely sweet and delicate flavor. It doesn't taste at all like huckleberries or blueberries.

Fortunately, serviceberries ripen in late July and early August—about the same time as early blueberries and huckleberries. If a berry picker takes along an extra bucket, then he or she can pick both berries on the same trip.

One of the biggest shortcomings of serviceberries is that birds love them. Since serviceberries ripen sequentially, a bush that contains 100 berries might only have ten ripe at one time. Birds (and bears, for that matter) can rummage from bush to bush and keep up with the ripening berries. It's only in exceptional years that a picker can obtain enough serviceberries to make a pie or batch of jelly.

Don't get me wrong. If you can pick a handful of serviceberries, you have the makings for a fine topping on your morning cold cereal, or you can add a little sugar and cover them with milk and have a tasty treat right then. You might not even want to wait for that milk and sugar, as serviceberries don't need any help; their sweet taste can give a hiker, angler, or mountain biker a great trail snack.

One time I found a big serviceberry bush along one of my day hike routes. The bush was probably 12 feet tall and had a diameter of 6 feet. There must have been five hundred serviceberries in various stages of ripeness on the bush, though most were still green. I noted that there were plenty of fuchsia-colored berries present and reckoned that they would be ripe in four days, so I made it a point to visit the bush then.

When I arrived four days later, I was surprised to see that there were very few ripe serviceberries and about the same number as before of the fuchsia-colored ones. I picked eight or ten ripe berries and was slowly eating them when a cedar waxwing lit on the top of the bush and started going from clump to clump. It ate what few ripe serviceberries I was unable to reach and flew off to the next bush. I figured that I wouldn't be able to compete with a full-time resident berry picker, so I stopped trying.

About three weeks later, I was doing a berry clinic for the Federation of Fly Fishers and found a serviceberry patch that just wouldn't quit. My class and I were able to pick 8 gallons of berries from the patch in spite of competition from the birds and at least one bear (scat was all over the patch). Now that was a productive patch!

I D E N T I F I C A T I O N

Serviceberry varies in height from 3 to 15 feet. The bark is smooth with a slight reddish tint on younger branches; the older branches turn a gray color. The leaves are deciduous, simple, alternately arranged—usually the front half is toothed. The leaf shape is oval, and the color a medium green on top and light green on the bottom.

Serviceberry is one of the first shrubs to blossom, in late April to mid-May. The people of the northeastern United States noticed that the shrub blossomed at about the same time the shad were on their spawning runs, hence, another of its names, shad bush. The flower is white and hangs in clusters, or racemes, of 3 to 20.

Serviceberry ripens from July through mid-August. The berries turn from light green to fuchsia to blue-black. The berries are usually larger than pea-sized to twice pea-sized.

Serviceberry prefers a moderate amount of sunlight and can be found in open areas, open woods (alder or aspen), hillsides, burn or logged areas east of the Cascades, and from sea level to mid-mountain altitudes.

In most years, if you can beat the bears and birds to a patch, you should be able to pick a gallon or more. The odds are about three in four that you'll be successful.

RECIPES

Stewed Serviceberries

2 cups dried serviceberries (from approximately $2^2/_3$ cups serviceberries)
1 stick cinnamon
$^1/_2$ teaspoon whole cloves
2 tablespoons lemon juice

Place berries in saucepan, cover with water. Tie spices in a cheesecloth bag and place in pan containing berries and water. Add lemon juice and simmer covered, 45 minutes. Use stewed serviceberries as a condiment for wild game dishes.

Darcy Williamson, Donnelly, Idaho
How to Prepare Common Wild Foods

Serviceberry Pie

pastry for 2-crust pie (see pie crust on page 124)
2 tablespoons flour
$1/2$ to $3/4$ cup sugar
2 to $2 1/2$ cups serviceberries
2 tablespoons lemon juice
$1/2$ cup water
2 tablespoons butter
cream
2 tablespoons sugar

Preheat oven to 350 degrees. Mix together flour and sugar. Stir in serviceberries. Line pie plate with bottom crust. Add berry mixture, then sprinkle with lemon juice and water. Dot with butter. Cover with top crust and prick in several spots. Brush with cream and sprinkle with sugar. Bake until juice boils up thickly.

Irene Willey, Huelett, Wyoming

Serviceberry Jelly

1 pound serviceberries
1 cup water
$1/2$ cup lemon juice
1 package powdered pectin
$4 1/2$ cups sugar

Wash and crush ripe serviceberries. Add water and simmer 15 minutes. To prepare juice, rest colander in bowl or kettle. Spread cheesecloth or jelly bag over colander. Place hot, prepared berries into cloth or bag. Fold cloth to form bag and twist from top. Press with masher to extract juice. Measure 3 cups juice into 6- to 8-quart kettle and add lemon juice and pectin. Stir well. Place over high heat and bring to boil, stirring constantly. Add sugar. Stir in well and continue stirring constantly. Bring to full, rolling boil. Boil hard exactly 2 minutes. Remove from heat. Skim foam and pour

(continued on next page)

into glasses. Attach lids and screw bands on securely. Place in boiling water bath for 10 minutes.

Yield: five to six 8-ounce jars

Bob Krumm, Sheridan, Wyoming

Serviceberry Waffles

$1\frac{1}{2}$ cups dried serviceberries (from approximately 2 cups of serviceberries)
$1\frac{1}{2}$ cups buttermilk
2 eggs, beaten
$\frac{1}{4}$ cup vegetable oil
1 cup whole wheat flour
$\frac{1}{2}$ cup white flour
1 tablespoon baking powder
$\frac{1}{2}$ teaspoon baking soda
$1\frac{1}{2}$ tablespoons sugar

Soak serviceberries 1 to $1\frac{1}{2}$ hours in 2 cups of warm water. Drain well. Beat together buttermilk, eggs and oil. Sift dry ingredients together. Slowly beat into milk mixture. Fold in berries and bake in greased waffle iron until done.

Darcy Williamson, Donnelly, Idaho
How to Prepare Common Wild Foods

Steamed Serviceberry Pudding

I cup fresh serviceberries
I cup sliced peaches
$^1/_4$ cup granulated sugar
$^1/_2$ teaspoon cinnamon
$^1/_3$ cup biscuit mix
$^1/_3$ cup granulated sugar
$^1/_3$ cup milk

Mix together berries, peaches, sugar, and cinnamon. Spoon into large custard cups. Make batter from biscuit mix, sugar, and milk. Drop onto fruit. Place in large kettle on rack with enough water to reach bottom of custard dishes. Cover tightly and steam on medium heat 45 minutes.

Darcy Williamson, Donnelly, Idaho
How to Prepare Common Wild Foods

Serviceberry Meringue Pie

I quart water
$^3/_4$ cup sugar
2 cups serviceberries
I teaspoon vanilla

To prepare serviceberry juice, combine the above ingredients and cook until serviceberries are plump. Simmer 3 more minutes. Remove from heat. Cool for 30 minutes. Crush the serviceberries, then send through a sieve.

I tablespoon gelatin
$^1/_4$ cup cold water
I cup serviceberry juice
$^1/_2$ teaspoon salt
4 egg yolks, well beaten
4 egg whites, beaten stiff
$^1/_2$ cup sugar
I baked pie crust (see pie crust recipe on page 124)
whipped cream

(continued on next page)

Soften gelatin in cold water. Set aside. In the top of a double boiler place serviceberry juice and add salt. Stir in egg yolks. Set the pan over the hot water and cook the custard, stirring constantly until it coats the spoon. Add the gelatin to the hot custard and stir until dissolved. Sieve into a cold bowl to cool.

Beat egg whites with sugar until they are very stiff. Fold the meringue into the serviceberry custard. There is no baking after the egg whites are added. Pour into baked pie crust. Decorate with whipped cream topping.

Alma Snell, Fort Smith, Montana

Strawberry

It seems that I have picked strawberries ever since I can remember. My parents used to have a big patch of strawberries. On the weekends we would pick strawberries and sell them at a roadside stand consisting of a card table and a small sign. People would always stop and buy the quarts of strawberries my mother had heaped up — she didn't want to cheat anyone. When a person bought a quart of our strawberries, they got a quart.

Those tame strawberries were many times bigger than the wild strawberries that I find in the foothills and mountains nowadays, but I don't think they were any tastier.

This summer I was guiding a father-son pair, David and Will, along a mountain stream. As is my habit, I don't fish when I'm working but help my anglers with tips on where to cast, how to cast, what fly to use, and how to approach a certain piece of water.

Both father and son were accomplished anglers so I really didn't have much advice to give. My eye wandered over the alpine meadow that the creek traversed. It didn't take me too long to recognize various wildflowers blossoming in the meadow. The bright yellow, red, purple, and blue colors contrasted markedly with the deep green grasses that abounded there.

I happened to gaze down and could scarcely believe my eyes. I had inadvertently wandered into a substantial wild strawberry patch. There were hints of red berries all around me. I did the only thing I could do: I removed my baseball cap and started to fill it with luscious berries.

It didn't take long before Will noticed me and figured out what I was doing. To my surprise, he put down his fly rod and started picking. We managed to pick a cup or so of wild strawberries and then headed for Will's dad to share our find.

I believe David considered picking berries a waste of time—time that could be better spent fishing. After he ate a few of the berries, though, I think his opinion changed, for later on I noticed him gazing down, seemingly in search of strawberries.

෫ක

IDENTIFICATION

Strawberries can grow in open, sunny areas as easily as shady woods, from sea level to timberline. Strawberries don't thrive in the desert; otherwise you'll find them throughout the Northwest.

Strawberries are a non-woody (herbaceous), perennial plant with a basal clump of leaves. The leaves are three-part with each leaflet having large teeth (dentate). The leaves are medium green on top and light green underneath with small hairs. The plants range from 3 inches to as much as 16 inches high.

At lower elevations, strawberries blossom from early May into June and ripen June through August. At higher altitudes, you might find strawberries blossoming in July and ripening in August. The berry is a miniature version of our garden variety strawberry. Most are slightly smaller than dime-size. If you find one that is nickel-size, you've found a real trophy.

Most of the time it is hard to come up with enough strawberries to make anything with. Your chances of finding enough for a quart are one in ten.

RECIPES

Wild Strawberry Preserves

I quart strawberries
3 cups sugar, divided

Pour boiling water over berries and let stand until water runs pink. Drain thoroughly. Put berries in a kettle. Boil 3 minutes. Add $1\frac{1}{2}$ cups sugar. Boil 3 minutes. Add another $1\frac{1}{2}$ cups sugar. Boil 3 more minutes. Let stand 3 days in earthenware jar. Stir completely, reaching to bottom of jar, each day. Put in canning jars cold. Seal with paraffin. The preferred method is to attach lids and screw bands and process in a boiling water bath for 20 minutes.

Nora Beckman, Port Hadlock, Washington

Wild Strawberry Sauce

2 cups strawberries
I tablespoon granulated sugar
I tablespoon margarine, softened
I cup confectioner's sugar
I egg white, beaten stiff

Place berries in bowl with granulated sugar; mash slightly. Beat together margarine and confectioner's sugar. Fold in egg white. Combine with berries. Good over ice cream.

Darcy Williamson, Donnelly, Idaho
How to Prepare Common Wild Foods

Strawberry Feather Muffins*

 $^1/_3$ cup sugar
 $^1/_4$ cup margarine
 1 egg
 $2^1/_3$ cups flour (some can be whole wheat if you like)
 3 teaspoons baking powder
 $^1/_2$ teaspoon salt
 $1^1/_8$ cups milk
 1 teaspoon vanilla
 1 cup strawberries

Mix sugar and margarine. Beat in egg. Mix flour, baking powder, and salt in a bowl. Mix milk and vanilla in a different bowl. Beat wet and dry mixes into margarine mixture alternately. Stir in berries and spoon into muffin pans $^2/_3$ full.

Topping:

 $^1/_2$ cup brown sugar
 $^1/_2$ teaspoon cinnamon
 $^1/_2$ cup flour
 $^1/_4$ cup butter

Combine topping ingredients until crumbly. Sprinkle on top of muffins. Bake 25 minutes at 375 degrees.

Yield: about 1 dozen muffins.

*Can also be used for blueberries, huckleberries, thimbleberries, raspberries, blackcaps, and serviceberries.

Janice Scott, Casper, Wyoming

Wild Strawberry Slump

Slump batter:

> 3 tablespoons butter or margarine
> 4 tablespoons sugar
> $1/2$ cup milk
> $1 1/2$ cups flour
> $1 1/2$ teaspoons baking powder
> $1/4$ teaspoon salt

Cream together butter or margarine and sugar. Add milk and blend. Mix flour, baking powder, and salt. Add dry ingredients to wet; mix. Drop batter by spoonfuls into Bubbling Berries. Cover and cook for 10 minutes.

Bubbling Berries:

> 4 cups wild strawberries*
> $1 1/2$ cups sugar
> 3 tablespoons cornstarch
> $1 1/2$ cups water

Combine and bring to a boil in a heavy saucepan. Cinnamon or nutmeg may be added to taste.

*Blueberries, huckleberries, blackberries, raspberries, serviceberries, thimbleberries and salmonberries can also be used.

Charlotte Heron, Choteau, Montana

Wild Strawberry Sherbet

> $1 1/2$ cups wild strawberries*
> 2 tablespoons gelatin
> 3 cups cold water
> 1 cup boiling water
> 2 cups sugar
> 3 tablespoons lemon juice

(continued on next page)

Puree strawberries. Set aside. Soften gelatin in $1/2$ cup water. Add to boiling water. Mix in remaining ingredients, including remaining $2 1/2$ cups water. Pour into freezer tray and freeze until solid.

*Blackberries, raspberries, salmonberries, and thimbleberries may be substituted.

Darcy Williamson, Donnelly, Idaho
How to Prepare Common Wild Foods

Wild Strawberry Chiffon Pie

I baked graham cracker crust
I envelope unflavored gelatin
I tablespoon cold water
$1/2$ cup boiling water
$1 1/2$ cups wild strawberries
5 tablespoons granulated sugar, divided
$1/2$ cup whipping cream
2 egg whites

Soften gelatin in cold water, then add to boiling water. Cool to room temperature, then fold in strawberries sprinkled with 2 tablespoons granulated sugar. Chill until gelatin begins to set. Whip cream until it peaks. Fold into berry mixture. Beat whites to soft peaks; gradually add 3 tablespoons granulated sugar. Fold into strawberry cream mixture. Mound into crust and chill.

Darcy Williamson, Donnelly, Idaho
How to Prepare Common Wild Foods

Thimbleberry

T himbleberry conjures up thoughts of walks down a steep, winding trail in a pine forest. Eventually the trail crosses and then parallels a mountain stream, where small brook trout abound. The stream enters a narrow valley that is covered with thimbleberry bushes. There are literally acres of thimbleberries. During August, it's a treat just to walk through the valley picking and eating these tasty berries. It's as close to an idyllic situation as I can imagine. While picking most other berries entails stooping and bending, or standing on tiptoes and pulling branches down, thimbleberries are usually at belt height and in plain sight. To top it off, thimbleberry bushes have no prickles or thorns, so not only are they easy on my back, they're easy on my hands and arms as well.

Sometimes when I autograph one of my berry books, I'll inscribe it, "May your hiking trails be lined with lots of luscious berries—all at belt height." You can bet that I have thimbleberry in mind when I write it. Unfortunately, thimbleberries are a rather soft berry and tend to pack down when you place them in a berry bucket. Maybe it's just as well, because thimbleberries are a great trail food. A hiker can snatch thimbleberries without hardly slowing down.

Thimbleberry can occur in rather large thickets so, though you may only find four or five ripe per shrub, if you find a big enough patch you might be able to pick a quart or so. Your chances are fairly good—probably 50/50. Since some of the recipes only call for a cup or two of berries, I would say that you should be able to make something out of your thimbleberry foray most of the time.

IDENTIFICATION

Thimbleberry (*Rubus parviflorus*) is a member of the rose family and belongs in the same genus as blackberries and raspberries. Thimbleberry plants are erect shrubs with no prickles or thorns on the stems. The plants range from 2 to 9 feet tall, with 4 to 5 feet being the most common height.

The leaves are arranged alternately. They resemble large (as much as 9 inches across), velvety, maple leaves, and are light green in color with 3 to 7 lobes. The margins are toothed.

Thimbleberries blossom in late spring. The flowers have five white, crinkly petals with yellow centers. The flowers are somewhat like large strawberry blossoms (up to an inch and a half across).

Thimbleberries ripen mid-July through August. The berry looks like a flattened, bright-red raspberry that is roughly $^1/_2$ across.

Thimbleberry can be found in floodplains, timber cuts, open forests, shorelines, and brushy areas from sea level to 8,000 feet.

RECIPES

Thimbleberry Sauce

$1/2$ cup sugar
2 teaspoons cornstarch
2 cups thimbleberries
$1/4$ cup water
1 teaspoon lemon juice

Mix sugar and cornstarch in saucepan. Add berries and water to sugar mixture. Cook over medium heat, stirring constantly until thick. Cool. Stir in lemon juice. Store in refrigerator. Good on ice cream or angel food cake.

Darcy Williamson, Donnelly, Idaho
How to Prepare Common Wild Foods

Thimbleberry Fritters

1 cup sifted flour
1 teaspoon baking powder
2 tablespoons sugar
2 eggs, separated
2 tablespoons water
$1 1/2$ cups thimbleberries*
oil for frying

Sift flour and baking powder together. Add sugar, egg yolks, and water. Blend well. Beat egg whites until stiff, then fold into flour mixture along with berries. Drop dough from a tablespoon into hot (365 degrees) oil. Fry until fritters are golden brown. Sprinkle with confectioner's sugar, if desired. Makes 12.

*Raspberries (red or black), salmonberries, strawberries, and huckleberries may be substituted.

Darcy Williamson, Donnelly, Idaho
How to Prepare Common Wild Foods

Thimbleberry Jam

$5^1/_2$ cups thimbleberries
1 box powdered pectin
2 tablespoons lemon juice
$^1/_4$ teaspoon salt
6 cups sugar

Place thimbleberries in large (6-quart) kettle. Add pectin, lemon juice, and salt. Bring to hard boil. Stir in sugar; bring to a fast, rolling boil. Boil 1 minute. Pour into sterilized jars. Attach lids and ring seals firmly. Place in boiling water bath for 10 minutes.

Darcy Williamson, Donnelly, Idaho
How to Prepare Common Wild Foods

Thimbleberry Turnovers

2 cups thimbleberries
3 tablespoons sugar
1 cup shortening
2 cups sifted flour
$^1/_4$ teaspoon salt
6 tablespoons ice water

Sprinkle sugar over berries; set aside. Cut shortening into flour and salt. Add water, 1 tablespoon at a time. Form dough into a ball. Chill 2 hours. Roll out pastry $^1/_8$ inch thick. Cut into 3-inch circles. Moisten edge of half the circle and place a generous spoonful of sugared thimbleberries in center. Fold in half, making edges meet. Press edges together firmly and mark with tines of a fork. Prick the top of turnovers. Chill 2 hours, then bake at 450 degrees for 15 minutes.

Darcy Williamson, Donnelly, Idaho
How to Prepare Common Wild Foods

Thimbleberry Rum Cake

3 eggs, separated
$1/2$ cup cold water
2 cups sugar, divided
$1/2$ teaspoon grated lemon rind
3 tablespoons lemon juice
1 cup flour
$1 1/2$ teaspoons baking powder
3 cups thimbleberries
rum
$2/3$ cup brown sugar
1 tablespoon cornstarch
$2/3$ cup water
2 tablespoons butter
1 teaspoon vanilla

Beat egg yolks with water until light. Gradually add 1 cup sugar. Beat 2 minutes. Add rind and juice. Sift flour and baking powder together. Fold into yolk batter. Beat egg whites stiff. Fold into batter. Pour batter into two round cake pans and bake at 325 degrees for 40 minutes. Combine thimbleberries with $1/2$ cup sugar. Mash lightly. Sprinkle rum over cooled cake layers. Spread mashed berries over one layer, top with other layer. Combine brown sugar, remaining $1/2$ cup granulated sugar, cornstarch, water and butter. Bring to boil over medium high heat. Cool slightly; add vanilla. Spread over cake.

Darcy Williamson, Donnelly, Idaho
How to Prepare Common Wild Foods

Thimbleberry Pie

 I baked graham cracker crust
 I quart ripe thimbleberries (separate out one handful and
   rinse with lemon juice and drain)
 $^1/_2$ cup sugar
 2 egg whites, stiffly beaten
 I tablespoon lemon juice

Run thimbleberries through a Foley food mill until you have I cup of pulp. Heat pulp with sugar until dissolved. Slowly pour over egg whites, beating constantly. Add lemon juice and blend thoroughly. Place half of the mixture in the pie crust and sprinkle with a few whole berries. Then put the rest of the mixture in the pie crust and sprinkle remaining whole berries on top.

Pat Robinson, Port Hadlock, Washington

Berry Good Hints

Berry Good Hints: Cross Reference of Berries' Best Uses

SNACK BERRIES

These are berries you can eat "as is," without any preparation.

Blackberries
Blueberries and Huckleberries
Raspberry, Red and Black
Salmonberry
Serviceberry
Strawberry
Thimbleberry

PIE BERRIES

Blackberry
Blueberry
Chokecherry and Bitter Cherry
Elderberry
Gooseberry
Huckleberry
Raspberry, Red and Black
Serviceberry
Thimbleberry

EVELYN'S BEST PIE CRUST

1 teaspoon salt
1 tablespoon sugar
4 cups flour
$1^3/_4$ cups shortening
$^1/_2$ cup water
1 tablespoon vinegar
1 egg, beaten

Mix salt, sugar, and flour in a bowl. Cut in shortening. Mix together water, vinegar, and egg. Add and mix thoroughly into the flour mixture. Chill in refrigerator at least 15 minutes. Roll out on well-floured board using well-floured rolling pin.

Yield: 4 crusts (enough for two 2-crust pies)

Evelyn Hejde, Aladdin, Wyoming

VERSATILE RECIPES

Blackberry Dumplings (Blackberry chapter)
Blackberry Cake (Blackberry chapter)
Blackberry Slump (Blackberry chapter)
Blackberry Juice Bars (Blackberry chapter)
Wild Blackberry and Peach Cobbler (Blackberry chapter)
Hobo Cookies (Blackberry chapter)
Trail Jam (Blackberry chapter)
Jelly Roll (Currant chapter)
Gooseberry–Thimbleberry Jelly (Gooseberry chapter)
Wild Raspberry Dressing (Raspberry chapter)
Very Berry Sorbet (Raspberry chapter)
Raspberry Sauce (Raspberry chapter)
Salmonberry Cake (Salmonberry chapter)
Wild Strawberry Sherbet (Strawberry chapter)
Wild Strawberry Slump (Strawberry chapter)
Strawberry Feather Muffins (Strawberry chapter)
Thimbleberry Fritter (Thimbleberry chapter)

CAMP RECIPES

Blackberry Dumplings (Blackberry chapter)
Blackberry Slump (Blackberry chapter)
Trail Jam (Blueberry chapter)
Gooseberry Dumplings (Gooseberry chapter)
Raspberry Pancakes (Raspberry chapter)
Raspberry Syrup (Raspberry chapter)

Calendar

	Blossoms	Ripens
Blackberry	May	July–mid-September
Blackcap Raspberry	May–June	July–mid-August
Blueberries & Huckleberries	late April–mid-June	late July–October
Cherries: Choke & Bitter	late April–May	August–mid-September
Crab Apple, Pacific	late April–May	late August–October
Cranberry, Highbush	late May–June	October–winter
Currants	late March–early April	mid-July–August
Elderberry	June–July	mid-September–October
Gooseberry	April–mid-May	July–mid-August
Hawthorn	late May–June	mid-September–October
Oregon Grape	April–mid-May	August–mid-September
Raspberry	June–mid-July	late July–mid-September
Rose	June	September–October
Salal	May–June	August–mid-October
Salmonberry	late April–May	mid-July–mid-August
Serviceberry	April–mid-May	July–mid-August
Strawberry	early May–June	June–August
Thimbleberry	late April–May	mid-July–August

Glossary

Alternate: a type of leaf arrangement with only one leaf per node on alternating sides of the stem. *See illustration on page 129*

Basal: situated at the base.

Biennial: describes a life cycle that completes in two years.

Bloom or Blush: a whitish, powdery covering of the fruit, berry, leaf, or twig.

Calyx: the green outer whorl of a flower composed of sepals. *See illustration on page 130*

Cane: a pithy stem such as is found in raspberry or elderberry.

Cultivar: a cultivated variety of plant.

Cyme: a flat-topped or nearly flat-topped flower cluster, in which the flowers blossom sequentially out from the center. *See illustration on page 130*

Drupe: a fleshy fruit with a pit or stone, e.g., cherry or plum.

Entire: without divisions, lobes, or teeth. *See illustration on page 129*

Escape: a cultivated variety of plant that has escaped cultivation and occurs in the wild, e.g., Himalayan blackberry.

Glabrous: completely smooth, without hairs or bristles.

Hip: a fleshy, cuplike receptacle that is the fruit of a rose.

Inferior Ovary: the flower parts arise from the top of the ovary. *See illustration on page 130*

Lanceolate: lance-like or shaped like a spear point. A long, narrow leaf that is several times longer that it is wide. *See illustration on page 130*

Lenticels: breathing pores in the bark that resemble warts or light-colored spots.

Mesic: the midrange of an environmental variable, e.g., moisture.

Node: a place on a stem where a leaf is or has been attached.

Obovate: tear-drop shape, inversely ovate. *See illustration on page 130*

Opposite: a type of arrangement in which two leaves grow on each side of a stem at each node. The leaves are opposite one another. Contrasts with alternate leaf arrangement. *See illustration on page 129*

Ovate: having the shape of a longitudinal section of a hen's egg in outline. *See illustration on page 130*

Palmately Compound Leaf: the leaflets arise from a central point. *See illustration on page 129*

Perennial: a plant that lives greater than two years.

Pinnately Compound Leaf: the leaflets arise along a central stem. *See illustration on page 129*

Pome: fleshy fruit from an inferior ovary, e.g., serviceberry and apple.

Pubescent: covered with soft hairs, downy.

Raceme: an inflorescence or cluster of flowers along one main stem. *See illustration on page 130*

Recumbent: lying on or leaning close to the ground. Trailing blackberries are often recumbent.

Render: to extract juice or pulp (cooking term).

Rolling Boil: a boil that does not stop when stirred (cooking term).

Sepal: a part of a flower situated beneath the petals. Sepals comprise the calyx and are often green-colored. *See illustration on page 130*

Serrated: having small teeth along the margins of a leaf or leaflet. *See illustration on page 129*

Sheet Test: a cooking term that refers to the jellying point. Take a spoonful of hot jelly from the kettle and cool a minute. Holding the spoon at least a foot above the kettle, tip the spoon so the jelly runs back into the kettle. If the liquid runs together at the edge and "sheets" off the spoon, the jelly is ready. *See illustration on page 130*

Simple: describes a leaf with a single blade. *See illustration on page 129*

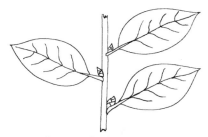 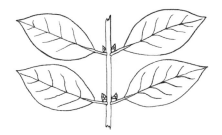

alternate leaf arrangement **opposite leaf arrangement**

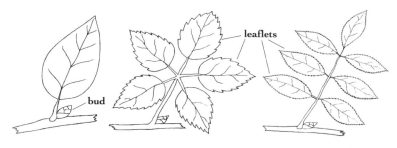

simple leaf
with entire margins

palmately compound leaf
with toothed margins

pinnately compound leaf
with serrated margins

lobed leaves

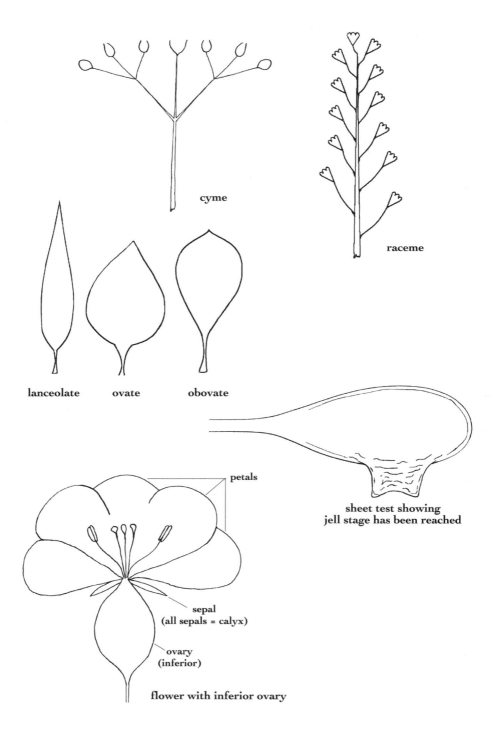

cyme

raceme

lanceolate ovate obovate

petals

sheet test showing
jell stage has been reached

sepal
(all sepals = calyx)

ovary
(inferior)

flower with inferior ovary

Bibliography

Brannon, Dave, and Nancy Brannon. *Feasting in the Forest.* 1989.

Furlong, Marjorie, and Virginia B. Hill. *Wild Edible Fruits and Berries.* Happy Camp, Calif.: Naturegraph Publishers, Inc., 1974.

Hitchcock, D. Leo, and Arthur Cronquist. *Flora of the Pacific Northwest.* Seattle: University of Washington Press, 1973.

Huckleberry Time. Gresham, Ore.: Mt. Hood National Forest.

Lewistown Chamber of Commerce. *Montana Chokecherry Festival Recipe Book.* Lewistown, Mont.: Lewistown Chamber of Commerce, 1991.

Massaccesi, Raymond. *Wine Makers Recipe Handbook.* 1971.

Pojar, Jim, and Andy MacKinnon. *Plants of the Pacific Northwest Coast.* Redmond, Wash.: Lone Pine Publishing, 1994.

Rocky Mountain Wild Food Cookbook. Caldwell, Idaho: Caxton Printers Ltd., 1995.

Savoring the Wild: Game, Fish, and Wild Plant Cookery. Helena, MT: Falcon Press, 1989.

Taylor, Ronald J., and Rolf W. Valum. *Sagebrush Country.* Beaverton, Ore.: Touchstone Press, 1974.

Underhill, J.E. *Northwestern Wild Berries.* North Vancouver, B.C.: Hancock House Publishers, 1980.

Williamson, Darcy. *How to Prepare Common Wild Foods.* Bend, Ore.: Mavericks Publications, 1978.

Common & Scientific Names Index

M

Mahonia aquifolium (M. nervosa, M. repens), 81–82
Malus fusca, 49–53

N

Nightshade, woody, 11

O

Oregon grape, 80–83

P

Plum, 13
Poison ivy, 13–14
Poison oak, 13–14
Prunus virginiana (P. emarginata), 40–48

R

Raspberry
  Blackcap, 26–30
  Red, 84–89
Rhus diversilobum, 13–14
Rhus rydbergii, 13–14
Ribes aureum (R. sanguineum), 54–56
Ribes divarcatum (R. inerme), 66
Rose hip, 90–93
Rubus discolor (R. laciniatus), 19
Rubus idaeus, 84–89
Rubus leucodermis, 26–30
Rubus parviflorus, 117–22
Rubus spectabilis, 100–103
Rubus ursinus, 19–20

S

Salal, 94–99
Salmonberry, 100–103
Serviceberry, 104–10
Shad bush, 104–10
Snowberry, 14
Solanum dulcamara, 11
Squashberry, 75–79
Strawberry, 111–16

T

Taxus brevifolia (T. baccata, T. japonicus), 12
Thimbleberry, 117–22
Toxicodendron diversilobum, 13–14
Toxicodendron rydbergii, 13–14

V

Vaccinium alaskaense (V. caespitosum, V. membranaceum, V. ovalifolium, V. ovatum, V. uliginosum), 33–34
Vaccinium parvifolium, 31, 33–34
Viburnum edule (V. opulus), 76

Y

Yew
  English, 12
  Japanese, 12
  Western, 12

Recipe Index